D0942294

I Remember Korea

I Remember Korea

VETERANS TELL THEIR STORIES OF THE KOREAN WAR, 1950–53

by LINDA GRANFIELD

Fitzhenry & Whiteside

Fitzhenry & Whiteside Limited
195 Allstate Parkway
Markham, Ontario L3R 4T8

www.fitzhenry.ca   godwit@fitzhenry.ca

Fitzhenry & Whiteside acknowledges with thanks the Canada Council for the Arts, the Government of Canada through its Book Publishing Industry Development Program, and the Ontario Arts Council for their support of our publishing program.

National Library of Canada Cataloguing in Publication

Granfield, Linda
I remember Korea : veterans tell their stories of the Korean War, 1950-53 / by Linda Granfield.

Includes bibliographical references and index.
ISBN 1-55005-092-3 (bound).—ISBN 1-55005-095-8 (pbk.)

1. Korean War, 1950-1953—Personal narratives, Canadian. 2. Korean War, 1950-1953—Personal narratives, American. I. Title.

DS921.6..G72 2003   951.904'2'0922   C2003-906407-7

Cover Photograph Credits
Front: Near Haktong-ni, Korea, an infantryman whose buddy has been killed is comforted by a fellow soldier. Nearby, another soldier fills in casualty tags to record the dead, August 28, 1950. (Sfc. Al Chang, U.S. Army. Courtesy of National Archives & Records Administration, Maryland)
Back: Bob Charlesworth (left) and his brother Don both served in Korea. (From the collection of Robert D. Charlesworth)

Printed in Canada

10 9 8 7 6 5 4 3 2 1

Although weighed down by his poncho and rifle, a statue of a Korean War soldier appears to stride across "rice paddies" at the Korean War Veterans Memorial in Washington, D.C.

With thanks to Scott L. Defebaugh
and the other men and women who came home,
and in memory of those who did not

Acknowledgments

I would like to sincerely thank my editor, Virginia Buckley, for taking this incredible virtual journey with me across the war-torn hills of Korea. It was an overwhelming trip through the past, which one neither wants to make nor can make alone, and I was buoyed by her wealth of insights, constant patience, and friendship.

Thanks as well to Russell Freedman, who brings to this project the eye of both a Korean War veteran and an incomparable factual book author. I am indebted to him for his foreword, and his wartime service.

Sincere thanks to all of the veterans and their family members who responded to my appeal for stories about, and photographs of, the Korean War. They have shared very intimate memories and have remained patient as I tried to understand "their war." I have found many new friends among these remarkable men and women. My respect for them has grown immensely during this process.

Special gratitude in particular to Scott L. Defebaugh, who discovered my books about World War I and II and subsequently invited me to provide another group of veterans with a book to share with their grandchildren. Others to be thanked for their valuable advice and assistance during this book's creation include: Clarion Books editor Lynne Polvino; James W. Kerr; David Bennett of Transatlantic Literary Agency Inc.; Janet Lunn; Hal and Ted Barker of the Korean War Project; *The VFW Magazine*; Vince Krepps, editor of *The Graybeards*; the National Archives & Record Administration, Maryland; Les Peate of the Korea Veterans Association of Canada Inc.; Timothy Dubé; and Gus Poulos.

Thank you as well to Dr. Jean Marmoreo; Tom Sammons; Bob Soesbe; Ward A. Weaver; Sam Carr; Jerry Welchert; Roger G. Baker; John W. Boone; Robert R. Kutcher; Susan E. Richmond; Paul G. Martin; James and Doreen Lyons; the Library of Congress Prints and Photographs Division; Susan Miller Cook; Christine Martin; Michael F. Dolan and his sister Meaghean; and Ted Rushton and staff members of the U.S. Department of Defense Korean War Commemoration Committee and Korea 50 Web site.

A special thank-you to Captain Duncan D. McMillan, Regimental Adjutant, The Royal Canadian Regiment, for his invaluable detective work regarding "Korea," the poem attributed to Private Patrick W. O'Connor. And lastly, heartfelt thanks to my family, Devon, Brian, and Cal Smiley, for their constant love and support, and their willingness to join me on yet another adventure into the past.

Contents

After the War

I Remember the Korean War

RUSSELL FREEDMAN

The Korean War is often called "the Forgotten War," but as the stories in this book demonstrate, no war can ever be forgotten by the combatants and civilians whose lives were affected and who were lucky enough to survive. Reading these stories helped jog my memory and remind me of my own experiences in Korea, of the sacrifices that war exacts, and of the questions raised by any war that cannot be easily answered.

I was a twenty-two-year-old draftee, fresh out of college and basic training, when I arrived in Korea and joined the Counter Intelligence Corps detachment assigned to the Second Infantry Division. Our job was to counter, or oppose, enemy efforts to gather intelligence about our division. In other words, we were supposed to keep the enemy from spying on us.

Shortly after I arrived, our commanding officer, Major Victor, discovered that I

Russell Freedman is seen here wearing the Second Infantry Division "Indian Head" patch on his left arm. His beret was given to him by friends in the French Battalion, which was attached to the Second Infantry Division (one of many U.N. units).

was an aspiring writer. Since the detachment was required to submit a daily report, writing that report became one of my assignments. Every evening I would sit at the typewriter in our headquarters tent and compose a detailed account of our activities that day. The reports had to be concise, accurate, and to the point, which was great writing practice!

The Second Division was stationed along one segment of the MLR—the Main Line of Resistance—where United Nations forces faced Chinese and North Korean troops across a narrow and hilly no man's land. By the time I got there in March 1952, the war had reached a stalemate, and peace talks were being held. Even so, fighting continued as the two sides exchanged artillery fire and mortar attacks, probed back and forth across the MLR, and battled over the possession of strategic hills.

Our CIC detachment had its own compound of tents some distance back from the fighting front, beyond the range of enemy artillery. Occasionally, a low-flying dive bomber would swoop over our area and drop a bomb or two as we raced to an underground bunker for shelter. Once or twice, the plane turned out to be one of our own aircraft dumping what was left of its payload after a bombing run over enemy lines. The opposing forces were so close together, and the planes flew so fast, that they zoomed from enemy to friendly territory in an instant and sometimes missed their intended target.

One of our jobs was to conduct security inspections of every unit in the division. If we ventured too close to the MLR on one of those missions, we might come under mortar fire. We also made occasional trips by jeep to CIC headquarters in Seoul, the Korean capital, where hollow buildings stood like skeletons amid heaps of bricks and ashes. But for the most part, we did not experience the dangers that confronted the front-line troops every day. The only casualty that occurred in our detachment during my year in Korea was suffered by one of our Korean houseboys, who shot off his thumb when he started to clean a pistol.

Another of our duties was to interrogate, with the help of our Korean interpreters, anyone caught within the division perimeter who wasn't authorized to be there. Most of the people brought to us for questioning were women or elderly men or even kids who had been innocently scrounging for food, and they were simply sent back behind the lines. We also were the initial unit to screen prisoners of war captured by Second Division troops. I'll never forget one Chinese soldier who was brought in just after he had surrendered. He was wearing a heavily quilted winter uniform and a fur cap with ear flaps, and he had a U.S. Army identification tag pinned to his chest. He was just a teenager, a peasant boy who had never been out of his village until he answered the call for volunteers to join the Chinese Communist Forces. Some POWs expected to be tortured or killed, and this guy, as he stood before us, was so frightened that he was visibly shaking. He couldn't keep his teeth from chattering. There wasn't much he could tell us, and we passed him along for further interrogation at Ninth Corps headquarters and, eventually, to a prisoner-of-war camp. I remember thinking as I looked at that shivering, shaking kid: Is this really the face of our enemy?

Still another function of the CIC was to plan security measures for visiting VIPs. During the 1952 presidential campaign, Dwight D. Eisenhower promised that if he were elected, he would go to Korea to assess the war. At the end of November he fulfilled that pledge, flying secretly to the war zone for a whirlwind three-day visit. Our detachment was responsible for making security arrangements the day that Ike visited the Second Division. I had no chance to make notes that day, so long ago, but as clearly as I can remember, here is how the visit unfolded.

Early in the morning, hours before the president-elect was scheduled to arrive, we went to the division airstrip to carry out our security inspection, Later we were joined by a large contingent of troops, soldiers from every company in the division, who formed an honor guard that would greet Ike. We waited in the biting cold for what seemed like a very long time until the small plane carrying him finally touched down. Flashing his famous smile and holding his hand up in a V-for-Victory sign, Ike emerged from the plane accompanied by General Mark Clark, commander of the United Nations forces, while we stood smartly at attention and saluted. Then Ike and General Clark climbed into a jeep, and we all set out in a convoy for an infantry company on the front line.

The day's activities had been planned and rehearsed down to the last detail. Ike was escorted to a nearby hilltop observation bunker, where he could have a look at the enemy lines, some distance away. We stayed behind, but we were told that the bunker had been specially outfitted for Ike's visit, including a generator-powered refrigerator stocked with soft drinks and beer. When Ike returned from the bunker, our convoy of jeeps took him back to the airstrip. He boarded his plane and flew off to visit another front-line unit, where he chatted with some GIs and had lunch with an enlisted man, a staff sergeant, if I remember correctly. Sitting side by side outside a tent, they ate their lunches from standard-issue aluminum mess kits as a Signal Corps photographer took several pictures.

A day or so later, a big photo of Ike and the sergeant eating lunch from their mess kits was featured on the front page of *Stars and Stripes*, the

Russell Freedman and Lim, a Korean man who could translate Chinese and served as an interpreter.

army newspaper. We heard that similar photos appeared in newspapers around the world. Unfortunately, we also heard some sad and unsettling news: we were told that the morning after his lunch with Ike, the sergeant had been killed as he led a patrol into no man's land. I never found out whether that was a rumor or a tragic fact.

My tour of duty with the Second CIC Detachment lasted for three more months. In March 1953, I left the detachment on my way to Japan and then back home to the United States, where I was discharged after my two years of army service. I had spent exactly a year in Korea and been fortunate to stay out of harm's way. I didn't earn any combat medals or Purple Hearts, but I was awarded three service ribbons to wear on my uniform: the Korean Service Medal, the United Nations Service Medal, and the Commendation Ribbon with Medal Pennant. I was especially pleased by that last medal; the citation commended me for writing outstanding daily reports!

I came home unscathed, ready to get on with my life. But I can never forget the sacrifices made by so many others: more than 54,000 American soldiers died in Korea, an estimated 700,000 to 900,000 Chinese troops lost their lives, and nearly three million Koreans—a tenth of the entire population—were wounded or killed during "the Forgotten War."

Introduction

For centuries before the birth of Christ, there was a civilization in the kingdom of Choson, or Korea—"the Land of the Morning Calm." This land of deep valleys and high mountains is bordered by China to the north and Japan, across the Korea Strait and the Sea of Japan, to the east.

For hundreds of years, Korea was ruled by Chinese or Japanese invaders. By the early 1900s, the country was under Japanese control. After the defeat of Japan at the end of World War II (1939–45), Korea was left with no government of its own. The United States and the Soviet Union (then friendly nations) agreed to help Korea—troops from the Soviet Union would help Koreans who lived north of the 38th parallel (an invisible line that divides Korea into almost equal halves), and American troops would help those south of it.

But the Soviet-American friendship was breaking down. The form of government in the Soviet Union was Communism, a harsh system with strict controls over people. Other countries were being influenced and controlled by the Soviet Communists. The United States and other nations worried that the Soviet Union's Communism might be spread all over the world, and they felt that some action had to be taken to prevent this.

In 1947, the United Nations called for an election in Korea so that the country would finally have a stable government. But the Soviets refused to allow an election in the north of Korea. The Soviet army trained the North Koreans, supplied them with military equipment, and then left. North Korea became known as the Democratic People's Republic of Korea, and its leader was Premier Kim Il Sung.

The south of Korea became known as the Republic of Korea and was led by an elected president, Syngman Rhee. American troops left Korea in 1949. By the end of that year, China had become a Communist nation. Joseph Stalin, secretary general of the Communist Party in the Soviet Union, and Chinese leader Mao Tse-tung (later known as Mao Zedong) had much to gain by adding Korea to their empire. Neither leader thought that the Western nations, especially the United States, would interfere if they moved into South Korea.

Soon after North Korean troops moved into South Korea on the morning of June 25, 1950, they learned how interested the rest of the world was in the fate of Korea. The United Nations demanded that they immediately withdraw, but the North Korean army remained in the south. The UN began to send aid to South Korea, and American army troops stationed in nearby Japan were ordered to help.

On June 30, President Harry S. Truman authorized the movement of more troops into Korea, but the United States Congress never actually declared war on North Korea. For this reason, the war, which lasted from 1950 to 1953, was often called a "police action" or was referred to as "the Korean Conflict." Later years brought attention to the Vietnam War and Persian Gulf war. Sadly, as the decades passed, the Korean War became known as "the Forgotten War," despite the fact that armed forces have been stationed on both sides of the DMZ (demilitarized zone) from 1953 until the present.

As the fiftieth anniversary commemorations of the Korean War began in 2000, veterans and U.S. government committees put a lot of energy and funds into making the world more aware of Korea, its war, and the service members who came home—and those who did not. Materials that introduced the war and its veterans were needed but were not readily available. The work on this book began.

Men and women from across North America responded to my invitation—published in veterans' magazines, posted on the Internet, and distributed to veterans' organizations—to share with young readers some memories of their Korean War experiences. Handwritten and typed stories arrived by mail. Some sent their stories and scanned photographs by e-mail. Others asked their sons and daughters to send their stories because they found them too painful to write. One contributor sent me an audio tape with her story on it, complete with chuckles and, at the very end, a voice broken by emotion. Unfortunately, some of the veterans have passed away since they contributed their stories.

Interest in the war has grown. Web sites celebrate the fiftieth anniversary of the Korean War. In fact, the Korean War Project Web site has nearly twenty-five thousand individuals on its mailing list. Despite this recent attention, a veteran wrote to me to say that it was difficult to find information about "his war" to share with his grandchildren and asked if I could help. As a result of his request, you will meet this veteran and others like him.

Both those who did and those who did not return from the Korean battlefields paid a price in "the Land of the Morning Calm." Memories haunt the survivors. Some of those memories appear on these pages, along with photographs from their personal albums. [Please note that bracketed information is material the author has added for clarification.] All of the stories in this book are true.

I Remember Korea

1 Reprßschmözes

Patrick W. O'Connor

"Korea"

PATRICK W. O'CONNOR

There is blood on the hills of Korea.
'Tis the blood of the brave and the true.
Where the Twenty-fifth Brigade battled together
Under the banner of the Red, White and Blue.

As they marched over the fields of Korea,
To the hills where the enemy lay,
They remembered the Brigadier's order:
"These hills must be taken today!"

Forward they marched into battle,
With faces unsmiling and stern.
They knew as they charged the hillside
There were some that would never return.

1

Some thought of their wives and mothers,
Some thought of their sweethearts so fair.
And some, as they plodded and stumbled,
Were reverently whispering a prayer.

There is blood on the hills of Korea.
It's the gift of the freedom they love.
May their names live in glory forever,
And their souls rest in heaven above.

Private O'Connor of Sarnia, Ontario, was a stretcher-bearer with C Company of the Second (Special Service) Battalion of The Royal Canadian Regiment, part of the Canadian Twenty-fifth Brigade and attached to the United States Twenty-fifth Infantry Division. A platoon commander remembered that during the battle at Chail-Li "Paddy came running up with the stretcher over his shoulder. He said, 'To hell with it. I'm going after my boys.' He was right beside me. We were all so close. All of a sudden, he was dead, shot three or four times. The stretcher and the first-aid kit hit the ground."

O'Connor had been in action in Korea only five days when he was killed. He wrote this poem on May 29, 1951—the night before he died. He is buried in the United Nations Cemetery at Pusan, South Korea.

Terror and Courage

1950

- Dawn, June 25, 1950—North Korean troops swarm over the 38th parallel, which divides North and South Korea, and march south to capture the capital city of Seoul. The Korean War begins.

- U.S. President Harry S. Truman orders American troops into Korea. The first soldiers land at Pusan on July 1, 1950.

- The UN asks the United States to organize the forces from Canada, Turkey, Australia, and other nations. World War II hero General Douglas MacArthur is named head of the combined forces.

- By the end of July, the North Korean army has overpowered the UN troops. The Pusan Perimeter, a zone surrounding the city, is established, and UN forces prepare to repel the enemy.

- In September, MacArthur's troops land successfully at Inchon and capture the port. The UN forces break out of the Perimeter, and the enemy retreats.

- Seoul is recaptured by the allied forces, and Syngman Rhee is once again installed as the president of South Korea. By the end of September, the North Korean army has been forced back over the 38th parallel.

- China threatens to enter the war if American troops cross the 38th parallel. Despite the threats, MacArthur moves past the Yalu River and into China. By the end of November, the Chinese army, on the side of North Korea, has caused UN forces to retreat.

- At the Chosin Reservoir, in below-freezing temperatures, U.S. Marines fight the Chinese Communist Forces (CCF). The marines are surrounded and have to retreat, but they fight all the way to the port city of Hungnam. In Hungnam, they join thousands of Korean refugees, trapped with the enemy army on one side and the sea on the other. Thousands are evacuated from the port and taken to safety in South Korea.

George Dawson was a veteran of World War II and, after eight years of service, was nearly at the end of his enlistment in the U.S. Navy. He was a member of the Naval Reserve and working as a radio operator at RCA Communications in New York City when the Korean War began. Within a few days, he was called back for full-time duty and was told that he would have to remain on active duty indefinitely. George learned that even nature can become the enemy during wartime.

Caught in a Typhoon

GEORGE G. DAWSON

I was ordered to report to a navy base in California, where I joined the crew of a ship that was an attack cargo vessel, designed to carry troops, vehicles, equipment, and supplies into the war zones. It made many trips to Japan and Korea during the year I was a member of the crew. The large ship carried several smaller landing boats that could be filled with men or matériel, lowered over the side, and taken ashore to support an invasion or some other combat operation.

My rating was radioman first class, and my job was to send and receive messages by Morse code. Serving on a navy ship is not like going for a vacation on a cruise ship. While I was on this ship, I experienced one of the most frightening events of my life. We were sailing in very bad weather. The sea was very rough, and the ship was rocking and rolling violently. It was almost impossible to sleep. We had to strap ourselves in our bunks, which we called "racks," to keep from falling out.

George Dawson

It became dangerous to go out on deck, and ropes were attached from the bow (front) to the stern (back) of the ship so that anyone who had to be on deck would have something to hold on to. The cooks could no longer prepare regular hot meals because of the violent rolling and pitching of the ship, so we ate sandwiches of cold meat. We could not have coffee because our mugs would slide off the tables.

It was very hard for me to do my job in the radio room. The typewriters that we used for copying the Morse code messages were bolted to the steel tables, but the ship was shaking and rocking so violently that some of the typewriters actually broke loose. Chairs had to be tied down to keep them from sliding all over the room.

The weather became worse, and we found ourselves in a typhoon. The waves were as high as the vessel itself, and water was breaking over the bow of the ship. Things that had been tied down on the deck, such as tanks, broke loose and were sliding around, making terrible noise and damaging anything they hit.

At one point, the main antenna broke loose. We could not send or receive messages without that antenna. As the leading radioman, I was the person to do something about it. I knew that it would be a very dangerous task, but I felt that I could not order anyone else to take on the job of trying to secure the antenna. I would have to try to do it myself.

I would have to climb up the mast, grab the antenna as it was whipping around in the wind, and secure it to the mast again. I soon realized that this was not possible. Anyone trying to do this would be killed or at least seriously injured.

I went from the center of the ship over to the side, where there was a railing. Holding on to the railing, I looked at the ocean. It seemed that the ship was standing still but the ocean was rising up toward us. Actually, the ship was leaning more and more to the port (left) side. I was sure that we were about to capsize.

First, I thought of my wife back in New York. I thought that she would be a widow and might never know what had happened to her husband. My second thought was that I was alone on that upper part of the ship, and I wished I could be down below with my shipmates. "If I am going to die," I thought, "I would like it to be with my friends." The ship remained in that dangerous position only a few seconds, but they seemed like an eternity.

Then, very slowly, the vessel began to turn upward again, and the ocean seemed to be receding from us. I breathed a sigh of relief and scurried down the ladder to the pilot house of the ship. The men there were pale and were holding on to anything that would keep them from falling. One of them looked at me and pointed to a device that shows how far the ship is leaning. He said that if the ship had gone only one degree further to the left, we would have capsized, and we probably would have all died. We survived this great storm, but the ship was badly damaged and eventually had to spend two weeks in port for repairs.

Many sailors suffered bruises and other minor injuries during that voyage. One man's condition was serious enough to require the services of a doctor, but we had no

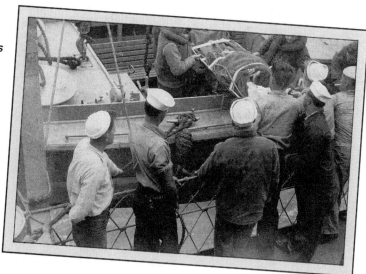

No doctor on board means this sailor must be transferred to a larger ship with medical personnel.

doctor on board. Once the bad weather was over, we secured our antenna and sent a radio message to a larger ship that was within a few hours' sailing distance from us. That ship agreed to meet us and take the sick man aboard.

When the ship came within half a mile of us, the sick man was strapped in a stretcher and placed in a small boat with several crew members. The boat was lowered to the ocean and made its way to the other ship, where the stretcher was lifted aboard. All went well until this small boat returned. Ropes were lowered from our ship and attached to the bow and stern of it. The boat was then slowly lifted up closer to the deck of our ship. Just as it was about to reach our deck, some of the ropes broke and the boat swung down. Several of the sailors fell into the sea; others managed to hang on to the ropes and climb safely on board. The boat was swinging wildly and then shattered as it bashed against the side of the ship. It took a great deal of effort to rescue the sailors from the water, but all were safely brought on board.

After the war, George Dawson went on to earn three college degrees, teach in New York City high schools, and become a college professor and dean. He is now a professor emeritus of economics.

Nineteen-year-old Eugene Inman had been in Korea for only four months when he was captured on November 30, 1950, in the Kunu-ri-Sunchon roadblock. For the next 1004 days, he would think only of survival.

1004 Days

EUGENE L. INMAN

The last week or so before I was captured had been difficult and dangerous. The extreme cold and the ambushes at roadblocks had cut us off from our own lines. We were out of ammunition and supplies. Eventually, my army outfit (Second Infantry Division, Ninth Regiment, First Battalion) was cut off by the enemy forces. As the Battle of Kunu-ri ended, there were many wounded and dead on all sides of us—on the hillsides, on the road, and in the ditches. The pass was blocked by a mass of destroyed equipment. We had to surrender, and did so a few at a time.

We were gathered up and placed in a holding area made up of animal sheds and vacant huts. There was no protection from the bitter cold in that mountainous area. The temperature was about thirty below zero. The wind chill drove the cold deep into our bodies to the point that it caused pain and restricted our movements, our thinking, and our reactions. The enemy removed from us whatever warm clothing they wanted. I was left with only lightweight clothing. My field jacket was the heaviest article I had; I also had a fatigue cap and a long, tattered scarf. I wrapped the scarf around my face and neck, covering all the exposed areas I could. My breath caused a layer of ice to form from my jaw down to my waist. That ice acted somewhat as an insulator, but there was no real protection from the cold. Rifles and machine guns refused to fire in the low temperatures. The oil in the trucks and jeeps turned to glue, and the vehicles refused to function.

We were forced to march under these frightening conditions for about fifteen days, from sundown to sunup. We walked without food, and as we passed, the civilians stoned us. Many of the stones found their mark and caused serious injuries.

The police and home guard were especially brutal. The wounded and the exhausted among us began to suffer. If a man fell out and could not go on, he was shot, bayoneted, or clubbed to death. During the march, we truly had no shelter from the elements, and the bit of food that was provided on random days consisted of cracked corn. Sometimes the corn was mixed with soybeans. This kind of food caused abdominal cramps and dysentery at all hours of the day and night. We were always thirsty.

In what I thought was December 1950, we arrived in a deserted mining town in the Pukchin area. This place was called "Death Valley." There we faced more bad weather, inadequate shelter and food, and death, as well as attempts to teach us how to be Communists. The fear, beatings, lack of proper food and water, and illness took a large toll in lives.

The huts and animal shelters we lived in were made of mud and stones and had thatched roofs. The inside walls were made of dried mud, and the floors were constructed of large flat rocks and mud. The rooms were extremely small, and we were so packed into them there was no room to stretch out to rest. Every time a guard wanted to express his anger on the march or in the camp, he struck, shoved, or kicked us in the arms, shoulders, leg joints, or backs. These areas never completely healed because they were re-injured by the repeated hits and falls we took when we carried heavy items in the slippery ice and snow.

We were fed only every twenty-four to seventy-two hours, and there was little change in food; like on the march, we had corn and soybeans, but with a little rice added on some days. Men died of starvation. Then the camp authorities added bean curd and seaweed to our diet and that helped the men who were not too weak to make a recovery. Malnutrition was very ghastly between January 1951 and August 1952. My ankles and legs were swollen, and I was always in extreme pain. This bone ache was not in the swelling but seemed to be in the very bones themselves; no rubbing or any other efforts could relieve it. Pain all day and leg cramps all night, then more heavy work the next day: carrying loads of wood and falling in the ice and snow. The endless pain drove me to argue with and

Eugene Inman, after spending more than three years as a prisoner of war.

resist camp authorities until a guard knocked out some of my teeth. I was made to stand at attention without shoes in the cold and snow until the guard was satisfied that I had learned to be humble and obedient.

Those of us who actively resisted this prisoner-of-war camp (and held on to our faith) were sent to a new camp. There they tried to break our morale and spirit; they attempted to make us suspicious of one another to break down any kind of leadership we had among ourselves. Up the Yalu River we went until we reached a place where we had to leave the river and walk. On August 12, 1952, we arrived at a place called Wiwon and set up a camp where we would exist and labor. In this new camp, the food and conditions improved because there were rumors of peace talks. Our death rate decreased, but our physical condition continued to deteriorate.

We remained at the Wiwon camp until we were moved south for our release at the end of August 1953, a month after the cease-fire was announced. I had been a prisoner of war for one thousand and four days.

I went on to become a teacher and school administrator. I married and have five children. I know that if we fail to recall our history, we will fail in our faith to defend it at all costs. We must relive our past tragedies in order to defend individual liberty, justice, and equal opportunity for all before the bar of God's grace.

Already a veteran of World War II, Edward Ziegler re-entered active duty in 1949. In 1951, a month after he became one of the first fifty helicopter-rated pilots in the U.S. Army, Ziegler was flying choppers in Korea.

"A Mechanized Angel"

H. EDWARD ZIEGLER

Because of my helicopter rating, I became the commanding general's pilot. I dropped rations, water, ammunition, and medical supplies to troops and flew regular observation missions. One of those missions is best described by a newspaper release and extracts from an official citation:

"Dateline September 1951, Heartbreak Ridge, Korea—Flame throwers were needed by the hard-pressed infantrymen who were stalled in their attack on the enemy-held bunkers on Heartbreak Ridge. Two were dropped by parachute . . . and a third was delivered via helicopter. The chopper landed almost 100 yards beyond the point of where the first two landed. The pilot got out and walked around to the passenger side of the chopper, unloaded the flame thrower, handed it to an infantryman who wanted to know what he was doing there on top of Heartbreak during a fire fight. Without answering, the pilot handed him the flame thrower and took off before the man could thank him."

I was the pilot of that chopper. In October 1951, the last hill was captured and Heartbreak Ridge was declared secure after 103 days of combat. The man I gave the flame thrower to was among the casualties of the battle.

In December of that year, I was transferred to the 8076th MASH [Mobile Army Surgical Hospital] to become a member of a helicopter detachment that flew med evac [medical evacuee] missions. We picked up severely wounded soldiers and flew from sunrise to sunset. Normally, there were no night missions because of navigational and weather problems, but sometimes I found myself following truck lights back to the hospital because a call had come so late that I couldn't get back to the hospital before sundown. We had no days off and we rotated missions. In the evenings, we helped out in the operating room wherever we could.

Helicopter evacuations were normally approved for the most serious wounds—generally head, chest, or belly—because those wounds would be aggravated by an ambulance ride. Any injury where time was a factor was always approved. Some fighting caused so many casualties that our whole detachment of helicopters was needed to respond to a pickup call. We passed each other going to and coming from the pickup point and the hospital.

Ed Ziegler

Sometimes, the clouds were so low and the weather so bad I was not able to fly higher than fifty to seventy-five feet above the ground.

On my first day of duty with the hospital, I was pressed into service to assist an operating team putting a cast on a Korean soldier whose left leg had just been amputated. I can't say enough about the dedication of the medical personnel who manned these hospitals. They were a hard-working group of people who worked around the clock when needed; an eighteen-hour day was not uncommon. They

A litter holding a wounded soldier is strapped to the side of the helicopter that will transport him to a MASH unit.

performed miracles every day in their operating rooms. Medical history was made and changed as a result of the procedures and techniques developed by MASH surgeons.

I can recall one evening in particular that demonstrates how skilled these surgeons were. Just as I was going into the movie tent with two of the doctors, they got a call to remove a "hot appendix" from a GI who had just been brought in. They insisted that I go with them and said, "If we are going to miss the movie, so are you."

I helped carry the man into the operating room. He was given a spinal. The doctors located his appendix, got it out, and sewed him up. I watched the entire operation and talked to the GI through it all, giving him a blow-by-blow description of what was going on. Then, we carried him into the postoperative ward. The operation took exactly eighteen minutes, and we were soon back in the movie tent. We didn't miss one scene of the show.

I visited the troops that I had brought in to see if they needed anything, to write letters for them, or just to chat. One of the troops named us "the mechanized angels."

You can't take that many well-educated, highly intelligent people and restrict them to an area the size of a football field and not expect some very unusual things to

Ed Ziegler and his ever-ready helicopter.

happen. Not all of the events depicted in the M*A*S*H television series (1972–83) took place, but many of them did.

One of the writers of the series was a friend of mine. He taped an interview with me and shared the information with the writing staff for the show. My wife, Alma, and I were invited to Hollywood as guests of the cast to watch the filming of an episode and have lunch with them. We met three of the show's actors—Alan Alda, Harry Morgan, and Loretta Swit.

I made several very good friends while flying for the MASH. We weren't members of a flight crew that painted fancy pictures or little bombs on their aircraft, but what we did was just as important. I am proud to say that I was a part of that mission.

Little did Hank Buelow know that the swimming and cold-weather work he experienced as a young boy would help him get through the Korean War's natural and physical challenges.

On the Battlefield

HANK BUELOW

The summers and winters of my childhood prepared me for some, but not all, of what I found when I landed in Korea in 1951. I was an only child, and when I was seven years old, my parents bought Diamond Point, a resort at the north end of Sauk Lake in Minnesota. Until I was twelve, I boarded with people in Long Prairie, about fifteen miles away, and spent the weekends and summers working at Diamond Point. I took care of the boats, acted as a guide, and cleaned the dance hall. I also learned how to swim.

At night, I cooked hamburgers at the dance hall during the intermissions, and by the time I was thirteen, I was a bartender and cook in the steakhouse. I spent my winter weekends and vacations sawing wood (using a two-man saw), putting blocks of ice into the icehouse, and assisting at the toboggan slide. Working in water and in the cold northern weather at Diamond Point helped me later.

I joined the National Guard when I was fifteen but was discharged a year later because they discovered I was too young. I re-enlisted in the Guard when I was seventeen and was eventually a tank driver. In 1950, I graduated from high school, and I was given a football scholarship to Colorado A & M (now Colorado State). I began classes there that fall. When I returned home for Christmas, I was activated as a National Guardsman, but because I was a full-time college student I wasn't required to go. I convinced my parents to let me. I was trained in rifle and small-arms use and had experience with floods (rescuing pigs, cows, and other farm animals) and labor strikes (protecting truckers from the strikers), so I felt I was prepared. In January 1951, I boarded the troop train in Long Prairie and got off at Camp Rucker, Alabama. I took ranger training and more physical training. I had ten days of leave to spend with my family in Minnesota before I shipped out for Korea in September 1951. En route, there was a two-day storm at sea and I worked on board with hipboots; I was the only one not seasick. There were rows of sick young men five bunks high!

We landed and marched into Inchon, Korea, and on to a replacement depot for a few days before we left for the Sixteenth Reconnaissance Company, First Cavalry Division. When we arrived at our squadron location, we were told we would be attacking the enemy the next morning and were asked if we had ever fired a bazooka. I said I had and was given one; this weapon later saved my life. Early the next morning, we left to attack Old Baldy (Hill 346), a huge hill that was several thousand yards wide and over four hundred yards high. It was bare dirt, with no trees, and was pockmarked with trenches, tunnels, and caves. We proceeded to one side and were to begin our attack when the artillery began on the top and other side. We were told we would not meet any opposition from the enemy. They were wrong! My squad started across a ravine at the base of Old Baldy, and I was directed to a small plateau and told to fire when I saw Chinese troops coming toward some flares. The rest of the squad continued on. The Chinese suddenly appeared with white flags, a sign of surrender, so I could not shoot. I had no signal to do so; our sergeant signaled to the men not to fire. All of a sudden, we were being attacked. The Chinese dropped into a trench and began firing on my squad. I could not fire because the Chinese were so close, and within seconds, my squad was killed. There was lots of noise and all kinds of shooting; I was in a mess.

I heard some yelling to my left and knew it was an American hollering for help.

I got out of the small hole where I was hiding and proceeded about thirty yards. I found a soldier with a terrible stomach wound. I held him in my arms and gave him a drink. He told me he was married and had two children. He was only twenty-three years old and was afraid he was going to die. I was, too. There was nothing I could do except holler for a medic. It seemed like hours passed, and a medic *did* come, but the soldier died.

A U.S. Army major general presents Hank Buelow (right) with the Silver Star for "gallantry in action."

The medic and I were in danger, so he left and I returned to my hole, got the bazooka and ammunition, and headed out. When I got to the Imjin River, I again heard someone calling for help. An American was trying to swim across the river and was having trouble. I jumped in and swam out. I was able to get him safely to shore. We lost 405 men and suffered 2300 casualties in only a few days on Old Baldy.

During my time in Korea, I had no problems with shooting at the enemy, man or woman. I threw grenades at huts where women were shooting at us; there were probably children as well, but we did not look for them because we were under fire. We saw villages that we had to burn out or that were already burned out. The youngest and the oldest people took the worst of it. At other times, we gave children the powdered eggs we did not like, and we shared candy and any other food we could get.

Besides fighting for our lives, we had problems with the rats and the diseases they carried. It was not unusual to hear rifles and pistols going off during the night as men tried to kill the rats in the bunkers. I had malaria, as did many of the other soldiers, but my work at Diamond Point helped save me from drowning and frostbite in Korea.

I left Korea in July 1952 after turning down a battlefield commission and a second tour of duty. My time in the National Guard would soon be over. When I returned to the United States, decorated with a Silver Star for one of the actions I was involved in, there was no parade, just a troop train home, a thirty-day leave, and my discharge.

Snakes could be as deadly as the enemy armies. Gus Wentz's job as a bomb guard may have been boring and not the stuff of heroic sagas, but it was an important link in the chain of defense that benefited everyone.

Things That Go Bump in the Night

B. A. "GUS" WENTZ

As soon as I debarked from the USNS *Mitchell,* the troop transport I sailed on to Okinawa, I heard the term "bomb guard" floating in the conversations. It was Sunday, March 8, 1953. We were heading on to Kadena Air Base. The next afternoon, when I went to my first duty assignment, I learned that bomb guards (BGs) were the men who guarded the B-29 planes that bombed Korea two out of every three nights.

The B-29s left Kadena in the late afternoon and returned to the base about four hours later. While the planes were on a mission, guards didn't patrol the assigned hardstands, the areas where the planes were usually parked. At Kadena, we had three rows of hardstands on each side of the three air taxiways. Not all the planes were needed for every mission. Those not used on a particular night were guarded so the enemy could not harm them.

Gus Wentz

There were usually so many guards working every night that anyone who didn't have a reason to be in the area had learned to stay away. A significant part of a guard's job was enduring the loneliness and boredom. We had to be alert and always aware of what was going on in a specific hardstand area. Any person walking around the area was checked out. Flashlights clicked on in the darkness and minutes later were clicked off.

We stood on guard for eight hours, alone, in the darkness. About halfway through our shift, coffee was delivered to each hardstand. Every man out there knew he needed that coffee to stay awake. It was far short of gourmet quality, but it kept us from going to sleep on duty, a very serious violation. The weather—quite cold, or very hot, and often very rainy—was something we BGs had to endure. But one of the real dangers out on the taxiways were the habus. These snakes were deadly, and their bite was usually fatal if not attended to within ten minutes. We were in the dark—fearing unseen snakes as well as the enemy.

As the hours wore on toward 2300 (11 P.M.), the sound of the six-by-six (a truck) bringing the relief shift was a pleasing bit of noise for those of us completing that evening's tour of duty. The truck stopped and then pulled away from each hardstand, delivering replacement guards.

If I had a different shift as bomb guard, I could see the first light of day over the South China Sea. I watched the ever-brightening sky until the beautiful red ball appeared on the horizon. Then it was time to climb into the six-by-six and ride back to the compound for chow and a much-needed snooze in the sack.

My memories aren't of great gallantry or brave deeds that won a battle, but they do represent a good number of guys who did their assigned duties and performed much-needed services during the Korean War. I am very proud to have served as a bomb guard through the spring, summer, and fall of the last days of "the Forgotten War."

As Lou Harmin escorted prisoners of war, he saw just how "like us" the enemy could be.

"Very Similar to Me"

LOU HARMIN

I was originally stationed in Japan with the Nineteenth Infantry Regiment of the Twenty-fourth Infantry Division. This army regiment and division went to Korea immediately after the outbreak of war in 1950. I joined them in April 1953 at the tender age of nineteen. I was assigned to Service Company and served my tour as a clerk/supervisor in the personnel department. I started as a private and finished up as a sergeant.

The unit was shipped to Cheju Island (Cheju-do) in July of 1953, just ten days before the end of the war. Cheju-do was used for two major purposes. The first was the basic training of the Republic of Korea troops. It seemed that if training was done on the mainland, the trainees were more apt to run away. On the island, there was no place to run.

The second purpose of the island was to be the site of prisoner-of-war (POW) camps for the Chinese soldiers who were captured. There were two prison camps on the island. At the northern end of the island, there was the camp for the Communist Chinese who wanted to go back to China. At the southern end was the camp for the anti-Communist Chinese who wanted to go to Taiwan. I was with the anti-Communists. They tattooed their bodies with anti-Communist slogans or with the flag of free China; others chose "Go Back Taiwan."

Once in a while, a Communist would pretend to be an anti-Communist so that he could get into the southern camp and spread his message. Such people were dealt with harshly.

The prisoners themselves were nice young men, very similar to me. Each morning, a detail of two Americans would go to the camps and escort ten prisoners back to the American camp. There, the prisoners served as workers during the day. I did several escorts. Two of us would take the bullets out of our rifles and then walk the ten prisoners to our camp. We then put the rifles against the tents, and the prisoners worked as cleaners, cooks, or in some other job where they were needed. One fellow would set up his barbershop, and I had many a haircut from him.

Lou Harmin

The prisoners made cigarette cases out of tin cans. They bartered with the American soldiers—a case for a package of cigarettes. The POWs also made rope and rubber sandals that we could "buy." I also remember bartering packs of cigarettes for fresh bread made in our bakeries!

Just before the war ended, South Korea's President Rhee threatened to have his troops release POWs all over Korea. We were put on high alert and given ammunition; our machine guns were set up on a beach to cover our retreat if necessary. Our role was to evacuate the area by sea, onto ships standing just offshore. In the end, nothing happened, and we were back at our normal jobs within twenty-four hours.

When the war was over, negotiations were made to repatriate the prisoners of war. Those who wanted to go to Taiwan went there; the others went back to China. My unit was sent to Koje-do and later to the Yangu Valley, just below the 38th parallel. I was home in August 1954.

Since the Korean War, Cheju Island has been renamed Jeju Island, and today, among Korean newlyweds, it is known as "honeymoon island."

During a war, every job is important. In all kinds of weather and terrain, railroad maintenance personnel like Jim Palsgrove had to keep the trains moving, delivering the wounded to hospitals for treatment as quickly as possible.

After the Battles

JAMES L. PALSGROVE

In 1949, the year of my high school graduation, I worked for the Baltimore & Ohio Railroad doing inspection and repair work. So when I was drafted into the U.S. Army in 1951, I asked if there was any railroad work available in Korea. There was.

After my army transportation training, I was sent to Korea in 1952. I remember our ship left Seattle, Washington, and on the pier, a band was playing a song with the lyrics "So long, it's been good to know you." When we arrived at the pier at Yokohama, Japan, another band was playing. This time, the lyrics included "If we knew you were coming we'd have baked a cake." A fishing boat eventually delivered us to Pusan, South Korea. From there I rode a Korean train called the Red Ball Express to Seoul. We were packed like sardines in that troop train!

Eventually, I became a member of the 765th Transportation Railway Shop

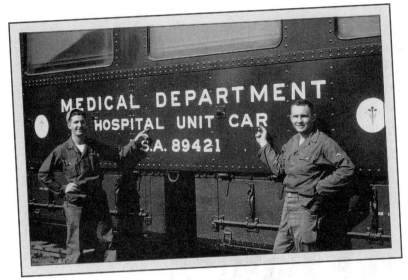

Battalion (T.R.S.B.) located in Pusan. We worked, along with the Koreans, in a back-shop there. A and B Companies maintained the railroad freight cars and the steam and diesel engines. I was in Company C, and we repaired hospital train cars that were stored at pier number one.

There were about five coal-fired hospital trains running between Pusan and the front. Each train had six cars, each with thirty-six beds for the injured soldiers. There was a kitchen car (and cooks, too) in the middle of the train. Huge steam engines, with Korean engineers, pulled the trains through the countryside and provided the steam that heated the trains and kept the water that was needed to run them from freezing during the cold winter months.

At first, I worked at the backshop and at pier number one, but later I was assigned to ride the hospital trains to the front lines to pick up the ill and the wounded. The trains were rotated to the front, depending on how much fighting was going on at the time and how many wounded needed to be transported to hospitals. On each train there was one doctor, one nurse, several medics, and one repairman, like me.

On a typical trip, we left Pusan and rode north to the front. Sometimes we had to wait on the tracks for a day or two while a train up ahead of us was loaded with wounded. If we had to wait a long time, we got out of the train and walked around the nearby countryside until it was our turn to move ahead.

If the train broke down, I had to get out, find the problem, and fix it as quickly as possible. Fortunately, I always had the part I needed!

After the wounded were loaded aboard, the train traveled south and stopped at different hospitals along the way. No operations were performed on the train; the doctor and nurse tried to keep the patients comfortable until we reached one of the hospitals. The hospital stops done, we returned to Pusan, where we cleaned and serviced the train. Then we went back up to the front, if there was the need.

Sadly, sometimes the trains stopped because they had run over people—civilians, who crowded the trestles along the way. The engineer would sound the train's whistle to warn them the train was coming, but they didn't always get off the trestle in time and the train couldn't stop quickly enough. Sometimes refugees tried to grab on to a train for a ride, especially when we crossed a river.

My work with Company C and the hospital trains continued until I left Korea in 1953. At that time, the trains were being readied for the prisoner exchange that would take place. (Later I found out the trains were used for R and R [rest and recreation]!)

The Red Ball Express spews thick black smoke as it chugs along between Pusan and Seoul to pick up injured soldiers. The thatched-roofed village and the stream are surrounded by barbed-wire fencing.

At Chorwon, above the 38th parallel, the wounded are moved from the tent hospital...

... to the army hospital train.

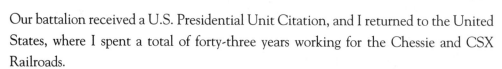

Our battalion received a U.S. Presidential Unit Citation, and I returned to the United States, where I spent a total of forty-three years working for the Chessie and CSX Railroads.

Little could I have imagined, when I was a boy and my father gave me an electric train set, that trains would take me into and out of war and into and out of railroad service for life.

Women of strength and determination, like Ruth Schairer, dedicated themselves to the rehabilitation of the torn soldiers brought to the hospitals. After valuable physical therapy, many were returned to the battlefields. Others, still too broken, were sent home.

Two Wars, Two Years, Two Weeks

RUTH K. SCHAIRER

I had been a member of the U.S. Army WAC (Women's Army Corps) during the last months of World War II, and I was one of the spectators at the Nuremberg Trials in 1946. During a break in the proceedings, I walked to the railing to look more closely at the German defendants. One of them, Hermann Göring, turned and looked right at me. I've never forgotten that look.

In the spring of 1950, I had completed my sophomore year at Tufts University in Massachusetts and was back home in Syracuse, New York, for my summer vacation. I had joined the 343rd General Hospital Reserve Unit in Syracuse and had been to a few meetings. But suddenly, war was declared, and the unit received notice. We were told that in two weeks we would be leaving for Japan, or Korea, or wherever.

On September 3, 1950, the 343rd was officially reactivated, and we were sent first to Pine Camp, now Fort Drum, New York. We spent only a day and a half at Pine

Ruth Schairer today.

Camp, and then we were put on a train back through Syracuse (we thought that was crazy) heading west across the United States. It was a nice train, with lovely accommodations and good food. The train chugged across the states. Some of us thought we were headed for Colorado, but we passed through Colorado. We ended up at Fort Lewis, Washington, right at the base of Mount Rainier, a mountain I now claim as mine, all 14,000 feet of it!

We were training at Fort Lewis from September 1950 until January 1951. Then we sailed from Seattle to Yokohama, Japan. The people in charge said they'd put us on a train to our next destination. We didn't know *where* we were going. It was a "milk train," stopping at every crossroads and waiting for other trains to go by. Instead of taking one hour to ride from Yokohama to Camp Drew, an air base near Tokyo, the trip took almost six hours.

We arrived at Camp Drew at night, and the mess was opened so we could eat. Then we settled down for the night. Everyone was so tired—we collapsed on our bunks and were soon sleeping soundly. When I awoke in the morning, I looked around and saw that everyone was sitting up in their bunks. "Boy, can you sleep!" they said.

"What do you mean?" I asked.

"Well," they said, "we've had an earthquake all night and you slept right straight through it."

That was my first night in Japan.

We sat with little to do at Camp Drew for about five months. Then I was sent into Tokyo to work as a physical therapist in a hospital. Our patients were UN soldiers from all over the world who had been wounded in Korea. The Turkish soldiers thought I was the best thing that ever came down the pike. They said, "We would like to take you home with us." That was because they liked big women, and I was

5'11" in my bare feet. I was a big gal. Because I was big, the local Japanese called me "Mama-san" and called the friend I was dating at the time "Papa-san." No matter where we went, that's what people called us.

The building where we were billeted was the Mitsubishi Main. Steel bars and heavy metal mesh were on the windows. The building was close to the canals and the moat of the Imperial Palace, and river rats could crawl up the walls. You didn't want one of those in your room! These rats weren't small like mice—they were huge, like cats.

By October 1951, I was back at Camp Drew, and we suddenly got orders to open up a hospital. We had two weeks (there's that "two weeks" again) to open a 1000-bed army hospital and be ready for our first patients from Korea. We did it, thirteen months after we'd left Syracuse.

Our patients were flown in from MASH units in Korea. We saw some horrible injuries, especially burns. The napalm stuck like glue on a person's body and caused deep burns. I worked in the physical therapy department, where some men were so badly injured they were still patients at Camp Drew when I returned to the United States the next year.

I had a choice of getting back home by boat or by plane. I chose to fly because I

Ruth Schairer as she appears (far right) in "Women Under One Flag Passing On the Tradition: Service—Honor—Courage" by Nancy E. Rhodes. The painting hangs in the Syracuse, New York, VA Medical Center.

had only ten days to cover the ten thousand miles to where I'd get my discharge. The first leg of my flight, to Midway Island in the Pacific Ocean, took thirteen hours. At Midway, they repaired the plane and put the rubber bands, or whatever they really used, back on the motors. My next stop was Honolulu, Hawaii, another thirteen hours away. More rubber bands. The last leg of my trip, to California, was another thirteen hours. When I looked down and finally saw the Golden Gate Bridge in San Francisco, I was absolutely delighted. I was home!

I had a long train trip ahead of me because I had to get to Fort Devens in Massachusetts to be discharged from the army. I arrived, stayed overnight, had my physical exam, and got my papers. It was May 1952.

We had lots of earthquakes and did serious work, but I wouldn't trade my time in Japan for all the tea in China. I saw interesting people and customs, and I'm glad I was able to participate in the war.

Noises aren't always what you think they are, as Arnoldo Muniz learned one cold dark night.

A Night of Fear

ARNOLDO A. MUNIZ

They were coming! I could hear them coming! The Chinese were coming! I couldn't see them, but I knew they were coming.

In the dark of night, I could hear them crashing across the small stream that lay between us—Tank Company, 224th Infantry Regiment—and them. I flipped off the safety on my rifle and dropped into a prone position behind one of our tanks. My eyes strained to penetrate the darkness. I searched for a target.

It was February 17, 1952, and the day had been a tiring one. The train ride up from Pusan had been hard and cold. At Chunchon, I reported to Service Company and was immediately trucked to Tank Company at Kumsong, North Korea. I was a tank mechanic, so I was in the right place. Even though it was late in the day, I was fed a hot meal, assigned to the maintenance section, and told I would be on guard duty that same night. My first night in Korea, and I drew guard duty. What luck!

Arnoldo Muniz

Beyond a small frozen stream, a feeder into the Pukhan River, rose some very steep hills. Somewhere hidden among those hills were two and one-half battalions from the 103rd Chinese Communist Forces (CCF) Regiment. Facing the CCF was our 224th Regiment, one of three that formed the Fortieth Infantry Division. Between the opposing forces was a horseshoe-shaped no man's land. That land was where Tank Company operated.

On that night, as I went on guard duty, the temperature was three degrees Fahrenheit. My post was to guard our motor pool and part of our sleeping area. I knew my job, but this was my first time under fire. Even as I slipped off the heavy mitten on my right hand, I could feel the fear ball up in my stomach and rise up into my throat. But then, as I dropped onto my belly on the cold snow, a certain calmness came to me. Thinking back to that moment, I still find it strange that terror and calmness could lie so close to each other within my heart.

I realized that the cracking, crashing noise I was hearing was just the frozen stream buckling under the intense cold. There were no Chinese attacking that night. I was witnessing a natural occurrence, one that a boy from south central Texas was not familiar with. I had just experienced gut-wrenching fear without painful consequences.

Later that night, after I was relieved from guard duty, I did not sleep very well. In the middle of that night, I prayed a lot. Korea had introduced me to fear, but in a larger sense, Korea had moved me closer to God.

There would be other nights of real, not imagined, terror. I was in Korea for nine months—and God was there with me. My war was one of long periods of great boredom with a few flashes of intense terror. I returned safe and sound to a nation that did not seem to know I had ever been gone. But I was not hurt, and my parents and sisters were very glad to have me back all in one piece.

Just as the war began, Willie Martin was called back into service with the U.S. Navy. He and the crew of the USS Bisbee *evacuated the wounded from Korean ports. Like many veterans, he wonders about the men they left behind.*

One of the "Train Busters"

WILLIE M. MARTIN

During one of the evacuations, we were close to the front lines. The ambulances were bringing us wounded boys whom we had to take to a hospital ship. Several didn't make it, and we placed them on the pier and covered them with blankets. Meanwhile, we continued to carry the wounded aboard. When we had to leave, the dead boys were still on the pier. I've often wondered what happened to them—if they were ever buried. I worry that they were just thrown off the pier. So many boys who fought in Korea are still not accounted for, and in my heart I feel that those boys on the pier could be some of those listed as missing.

After about fourteen months aboard the USS *Bisbee PF46*, I was transferred for duty as a ship serviceman second class on the USS *Orleck DD886*. I went aboard her in Japan in November 1951, and she set sail for the United States. After six months, the *Orleck* got orders to return to Korea. There we patrolled the eastern coast as part of the United Nations Task Force 77. We worked with other destroyers screening for our carriers, cruisers, and battleships, to protect them from the enemy.

One day, a plane from a carrier was shot up, and another plane was bringing the damaged one back in. As they got closer to the *Orleck*, we got orders to start firing at the two planes because they hadn't called in to identify themselves. We began shooting at the planes, and the pilots veered away from us. That's when we realized they were *not* enemy planes. Those pilots were lucky we didn't open up with our bigger guns.

On July 15, 1952, we were patrolling the Korean coast along enemy territory when we heard a train racing south. We sent up a star shell, and in its light we saw the train. Our big guns shot up the tracks in front of and behind the train and derailed it. The train's engineer tried to hide the engine in a tunnel, but we hammered it from midnight until daybreak. Planes from a task force carrier destroyed the engine. That enemy supply train had fourteen cars of ammunition, one car carrying tanks, and five more cars loaded with heavy artillery. You can imagine the sound of the explosions when the ammunition was hit. The USS *Orleck* and her crew became known as members of the United Nations' "Train Buster Club." Almost two weeks after the first train incident, we destroyed a second Communist war-supply train.

Willie Martin takes a minute to enjoy the sunshine aboard the USS Orleck.

After the attack on the North Korean train, we were told we would be buzzed by a celebrity. Sure enough, a plane flew within ten feet of the *Orleck,* and the belly of the plane was no more than ten feet above the water. The pilot buzzing us was one of the greatest baseball players of all time, Ted Williams! [A player for the Boston Red Sox, Williams served as a U.S. Marine combat pilot in both World War II and the Korean War.]

The USS *Orleck* was a great ship and a mother to the hundreds of men who served on her. After I was discharged in 1954, I missed her. You get attached to your ship. The *Orleck* was in service for the U.S. Navy for over thirty-five years. She served in the Korean and the Vietnam Wars. [In 1982, she was sold to Turkey and served that country's navy as the TCG *Yucetepe* for sixteen years.]

In 1999, the Turkish navy donated the USS *Orleck* to the Southeast Texas War Memorial and Heritage Foundation as a museum in Orange, Texas. The *Orleck* was built in the Orange shipyards in 1945—she is back home at her place of birth. The destroyer was towed almost 8000 miles from Turkey to Texas, and several of us who had served on her went to see her come into port in August 2000. I do believe we all shed a few tears to see her after so many years.

Restoration continues on the USS Orleck. *Visitors can tour the main deck of the ship in Orange, Texas, or visit her at www.USSOrleck.org.*

Hollywood's versions of World War II battles didn't prepare soldiers like Mike Schack for the dirt, the cold, and the decaying bodies they encountered in Korea.

Not Like the Movies

MARSHALL "MIKE" SCHACK

I served with A Battery of the Thirty-seventh Field Artillery Battalion, Second Infantry Division. Not long after my arrival in Korea in 1953, some of us were called to the communication bunker by our section chief. He said we were going to draw cards to see who was going to the hill as a replacement for a radio-telephone operator. At the time, an F.O. [a field-grade officer] crew consisted of a lieutenant, a reconnaissance sergeant, a radio-telephone operator, and a driver. F.O.'s were the eyes for the artillery.

Being kind of naive, I volunteered to go. I was sent to Supply, where I received a flak jacket. Then I was whisked away for the drive to Arrowhead Ridge. As I was led up the trenches and into the F.O. bunker, I began to think I should have taken my chances with the cards. There were only five Americans on the hill: a "sound and flash team" and the three of us on the F.O. crew.

It was not as glamorous as it seemed in the movies I had watched as a kid during World War II. The incoming mortar and artillery were scary and meant to do us harm. The hills were very steep, and walking in the trenches was even more difficult, although safer. Our driver brought us our mail, C rations, water, and ammunition. There were no showers or hot meals, just warmed-up C rations left over from World War II.

Mike Schack shares a moment with a child street performer.

We could get some of the Republic of Korea (ROK) soldiers to help us carry some of our stuff. We offered them the rations we didn't like—things like lima beans and ham, corned beef hash, and sausage patties. It wasn't long before the ROK soldiers didn't want them either! They liked what we liked—the baked beans and wieners!

We also encountered members of the Korean Service Corps (KSC), men who were too old for the army but who served as carriers. Occasionally, we found them going through our garbage dump for scraps of food. If we had extra food, we would give them some. They had no weapons, helmets, or flak jackets, and they were right on the front line.

One night, we were attacked by about two battalions of Chinese Communist Forces (CCF). The attack began early in the morning with a heavy barrage of mortar and artillery fire. The shells were exploding about every second. Our telephone lines were knocked out, and we had to use our radio to call our own artillery in. I remember being very scared.

The next morning, at daylight, I went down to fix our lines and saw my first Koreans killed in action (KIA). The Koreans had the bodies lined up in rice bags, waiting for a truck to haul them away. Seeing them made me realize how serious war was.

A battle was raging on our left at about the same time. We could see flares and firing at night. It was the Battle of Pork Chop Hill. A Hollywood movie was made about this battle after the war.

During July 1953, our Second Infantry Division was called up to relieve the Third Division. We replaced units on Outpost Harry, where parts of the Third Division had suffered severe casualties. We were given Third Division patches to sew onto our uniforms, and we replaced the division's units one at a time. But we didn't fool the CCF—on our first night on the hill, Chinese loudspeakers blared, "Welcome, Second Division. Nice to see you again. Soon you'll be taking a glorious journey home."

Harry was a bad place. There were bodies decaying in barbed wire, and we were so close to the Chinese that we had to disconnect the ringers from our field phones in case the Chinese could follow the rings to our exact location. We took some mortar, and a couple of firefights broke out from CCF probes, but nothing too serious. But it was there that I saw my first American wounded and dead. These bothered me more than the KIAs had on Arrowhead. Maybe I identified more with the GIs.

On the night of July 27, 1953, the cease-fire occurred at ten o'clock. Just before that hour, we fired all our ammunition so we wouldn't have to carry it with us. This caused so much noise that it was really eerie when the firing stopped.

We went back up on Harry to clean up and pack our belongings. I looked over at

Housecleaning at Outpost Harry. Anyone care for a rat?

40

the Chinese-occupied hills and saw the people waving at us. We waved back. Everyone was happy the war was over and we would be going home.

Suddenly, there was a very large explosion by our MLR, or Main Line of Resistance [now called the demilitarized zone, or DMZ]. We thought at first that the war had started all over

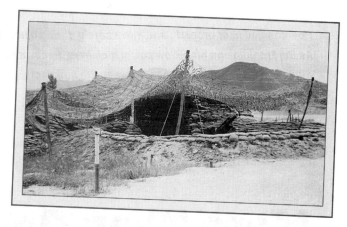

Gun pits surrounded with sandbags and lots of netting above provide camouflage for the soldiers and weapons within.

again. It turned out to be an ammunition dump accident. Five men were killed and several were wounded. It was a shame, because they had made it through the war, only to die in an accident after the cease-fire.

We moved back to new positions about two thousand yards away and began a new phase of our tour. Our unit and others "adopted" Korean villages to help them out. We wrote home and asked for clothes and school supplies, even though their schools weren't much more than makeshift buildings. When we took the gifts to the villagers, the children put on plays and danced and even sang songs in English.

The clothing was handed out from the back of a truck. The women and children were so anxious to get the clothes that they stormed the truck. We couldn't keep everybody in line, so we had to toss the clothes from the truck. Women grappled for each piece.

We had graham crackers for the children, but when we started toward them, they just rushed us and grabbed the crackers. This caused the crackers to break and crumble onto the ground. A lot of graham crackers were wasted. We should have handled the distribution differently, but we meant well.

I wonder what the Koreans' memories of that time are like. Today, fifty years after the war, soldiers still face each other from across the DMZ. Nothing much has changed.

How can you hear properly and move safely during a noisy rainstorm?
As Baj Franklin and his fellow patrol members discovered, a trusted
guide can mean the difference between life and death.

More Than One Kind of Enemy

B. A. J. "BAJ" FRANKLIN

When it rained in Korea, a small trickling creek could become a raging river in a few hours. Just such a terror happened to us on a standing patrol we went out on. I was a sergeant in the First Battalion, Princess Patricia's Canadian Light Infantry (Ninth Platoon, C Company) in 1952. A standing patrol was sent out to watch the bridges and roads that the enemy might use to approach our location. We would give an early warning of enemy troop movements and would change our position or withdraw if forced to do so; we did not have to defend our post. If the enemy were about to attack, we would hear their signals. Bugles and whistles screamed or the soldiers beat wooden sticks together.

On this one occasion, a small creek flowed in front of our lines, between us and no man's land. Led by our pioneer guide, we walked through our minefield and crossed the ankle-deep creek. We then advanced to our standing-patrol positions on

42

a high hill. It was raining. Our guide, my signaler, and I took our positions in an old bunker in the center of the location. The bunker was infested with rats, and we pulled our socks up over our trousers so the rats wouldn't crawl up our legs.

The rain intensified throughout the night. It was extremely difficult to see or hear anything because of the darkness and the noise of the heavy sheets of rain. At one in the morning, our commanding officer, Lieutenant Colonel John R. Cameron, was becoming concerned. He was receiving reports that the creek between our patrol position and our company lines had become a river. Because the waters were still rising, he gave orders for our patrol to return to the lines before we were cut off by the water.

Baj Franklin prepares to go out on standing patrol.

A close look at the laundry hanging to dry outside this house shows that someone is earning income by washing soldiers' uniforms.

On these standing patrols, a pioneer guide or a sniper led us to our position and back again. We appreciated their skill in guiding us through and past deadly obstacles. On this same night, we were glad to have Corporal Cassalman as our guide. As we moved back to our lines, we found the trails had become very slippery. Our signaler slipped and fell down the side of the hill. With great difficulty, Corporal Cassalman and I got the signaler back up the hill and on the trail. I told the other men to hang on to one another's webbed belts and hoped that no one else would slide down the muddy hill.

When we arrived at the place where we had crossed the creek just a few hours before, we found a churning river. Corporal Cassalman helped us through the waist-high, swift water and led us back through the minefield to our company lines—and safety. It continued to rain. We were each greeted with a shot of rum by company Sergeant Major Ashton Cliffton. That bit of rum warmed us as we stood there soaking wet and bitterly cold.

In war, one has to combat not only the enemy but also the elements. Quick thinking and equally quick actions meant the difference between life and death for troops.

Food, Fun, and Finally Rest

1951

◆ The war drags on with advances and retreats by both the North Korean and Chinese armies in the north and the UN troops in the south. Seoul is again recaptured by the Chinese. The capital's buildings are in ruins.

◆ The Battle of Chipyong-ni marks the first mass assault of the Chinese Communist Forces. The Siege of Wonsan lasts for 861 days and becomes the longest siege of a port in U.S. naval history.

◆ The largest single battle of the Korean War, the First Spring Offensive, occurs.

◆ General MacArthur wants to take the war into China. Everyone fears that if China is attacked, the Soviet Union will send its own troops into what could become a third world war. In April, MacArthur is relieved of his command by President Truman.

- General Matthew B. Ridgway, a World War II veteran, replaces MacArthur.

- In May, tired UN forces once again recapture Seoul. Landmark battles such as Kap'yong, the Punchbowl, Bloody Ridge, and Heartbreak Ridge are fought.

- Peace talks between North Korea and the UN begin on July 10, 1951, in Kaesong, South Korea, near the 38th parallel. No one can agree on anything, and the fighting continues.

- More peace talks take place in Panmunjom, on the 38th parallel. In November, both sides agree to establish the 38th parallel as the official border between North and South Korea. The debate about whether or not prisoners will be returned lasts for fourteen months. To some, this is still war—a "talking war."

Often, memories of war bring back horrible images, but sometimes a veteran can chuckle when he thinks about small changes the war made in his life, as Jim Ramsay does here.

Lima Beans? No, Thanks!

JIM RAMSAY

I enlisted in August 1950, two weeks after my eighteenth birthday. I was a machine-gunner in the Second Battalion, Princess Patricia's Canadian Light Infantry (PPCLI). We were the first Canadian battalion sent to Korea, and we arrived in December 1950, when some people thought the war was nearly over. But it wasn't.

During January 1951, we trained at Miryang, near Taegu. I saw trains overcrowded with Koreans, clustered like grapes, hanging from the cars. Some of the people froze to death riding on the roofs of the trains. They were fleeing from the Chinese troops. Conditions were terrible; sometimes what you thought was a pile of snow at the side of the road was a snow-covered mother and her children who had frozen to death. I also remember a line of Korean men in their white traditional clothing marching to Pusan so that they wouldn't be conscripted by the Chinese army.

In April 1951, we fought at the Battle of Kap'yong and, with the Third Royal Australian Regiment, received the U.S. Presidential Unit Citation for our defense of the valley. I lived in holes in the ground for almost a year—I was in Korea for three hundred and sixty-four days and came home in December 1951.

During our time in Korea, we survived on C rations. The civilians being evacuated were emaciated, and we gave them some of our food, mainly the cans of ham and lima beans. A box containing C rations held three cans of food, some hard crackers, a piece of Chiclets chewing gum, and some dehydrated coffee that we traded with the British soldiers for tea. There was a can opener, and a heat tablet to use to warm your food. The green cans had black writing that identified the contents: hamburgers and gravy, spaghetti and meat balls, or ham and lima beans.

Everyone hated the ham and lima beans. You could tell where we Canadian troops had been, because we left behind the unopened cans. The beans were salty and tasted like sawdust. We couldn't even use the rations for trading after a while. At first, when we wanted to trade with the civilians for services—let's say, to trade with a Korean woman for doing our laundry—we offered the ham and lima beans in exchange. Since the civilians didn't speak English, we developed a sign language for our trading—number one (one finger held up) was "good" and number ten (both hands up) was "bad." When we offered the cans of ham and lima beans, we saw lots of tens! We couldn't give those cans away. I haven't eaten lima beans since the war.

Remember, we were eighteen years old, and still growing. We were always hungry. If we gave up our can of ham and lima beans, that was a loss of one-third of our rations. There was no replacement food when you decided you didn't like part of the menu.

Jim Ramsay

Some food we did get excited about. My favorite of the C rations was the can of hamburgers. In each can, there were three or four burgers and thick brown gravy. A box marked "C-5" meant food for five men. Inside was a huge can, with maybe five pounds of bacon in it. That was great; but eggs were not available to go with the bacon. There weren't any chickens around. The North Koreans had moved south through the country, then the UN troops moved north, and then the Chinese moved south. By the time we Canadians arrived, the villages had been destroyed, and there were no edible animals around, although we did eat mule once.

A wounded Chinese army mule from Manchuria died, and we needed the food. Our machine-gunner group had a rifle company with them. We told this rifle company that the meat was beef from an ox, and we watched them try out this new dish. Half an hour later, the riflemen were still chewing on the meat. So we adapted our recipe, cut the meat into miniscule pieces, and made a stew. We ate it, but it was like chewing leather.

Still, it was better than ham and lima beans!

Sometimes all the service members needed to bring a smile to their faces was a pretty girl who could sing or an actor like Danny Kaye, who could toss off a few jokes and offer some time away from the battlefield. Scott Defebaugh helped this magic happen.

Something to Enjoy

SCOTT L. DEFEBAUGH

During World War II, I was a hospital corpsman, and after my separation from active duty, I signed up for the U.S. Army Reserve. I enrolled in college (thanks to the GI Bill) and worked several jobs while I attended classes.

In 1949, a hospital train unit was formed of army reservists in the Enid, Oklahoma, area; I became their supply person. I graduated from college in June 1950 and signed a contract to teach ninth-grade English in Woodward, Oklahoma. I was looking forward to beginning work on a master's degree, too. But my army reserve unit was activated the same day I was to have reported to teach. My unit was sent to the Presidio in San Francisco.

Eight months later, at the age of twenty-eight, I applied for and received a commission as a second lieutenant in the Army Medical Service Corps. Two months later, I was on my way to Korea. I arrived in August 1951 and was assigned to the Twenty-fourth Medical Battalion of the Twenty-fourth Infantry Division.

Because I was new to the battalion, I was assigned to many jobs, including battalion supply officer, motor officer, pay officer, assistant division medical supply officer—and "other duties as assigned."

The motor pool consisted of jeeps, trucks, and thirty ambulances that received patients at

Scott Defebaugh poses in front of a field of trucks, jeeps, equipment, and smokey fires.

the battle sites and brought them back to medical battalion clearing platoons for treatment and/or evacuation. The wounded who were classified as serious were taken by helicopter to MASH units. Other patients were taken by ambulance to a field hospital or treated and returned to duty.

All the personnel were housed in tents, which were heated by oil stoves that were turned off when we went to bed for fear of fire. Sometimes it was fourteen degrees below zero. Our lighting was provided by gasoline-powered generators. Both the heat and the lights were much more than the troops standing in foxholes had, and they were only two or three miles to the north of us.

Whenever conditions allowed, entertainment was provided for the combat troops. There were bands and variety shows made up of military personnel assigned to Special Services. Civilian entertainers, sponsored by the United Service Organizations (USO) or the Department of the Army, also sometimes came.

In November 1951, the medical battalion was asked to provide transportation for entertainer Danny Kaye and his USO troupe for the two days they were to visit us. As the motor officer, I was one of the drivers. The first day, their show for us was rained out. The performers stayed at our medical battalion, and we had a portable shower unit that Kaye and the others could use. (The water in the shower was pumped through a hose from a hole that was fed by a small stream. The water passed

Thousands of GIs fill the hillside waiting for...

...Danny Kaye and friends to share some jokes, music, and dancing with them.

through a heater and into the showerheads set up in a tent. The water was recycled over and over; it was not purified and was often soapy. Sometimes we needed to use fresh water from our canteens to rinse the soap residue off. Most of the time, at night, I filled my helmet with water and heated it on our tent stove. I bathed in that, and used the water for shaving, too.)

The advertising for the show was done by field phone and word-of-mouth. When we received the news that an entertainment troupe was coming, word spread quickly from foxhole to foxhole. A small temporary stage was set up just behind the front lines and decorated with pine boughs. The Twenty-fourth Division's special services unit supplied a battery-powered public address system that provided more volume than quality. Before the two-hour show began, Danny Kaye stood behind the stage talking with the regimental commander. He looked up and saw a long line of troops carrying their rifles and coming single file down the path. The troops were leaving their foxholes during a brief lull in the fighting. The colonel assured Kaye that it was safe to be performing, even with the men watching the show instead of being out in the field.

On that cold, overcast day, there were more than five thousand troops in the audience. They sat on the ground or up on the hillside. When everyone was settled, Kaye opened the show by going to the microphone, looking at his large audience, and shouting, "Who's holding back the enemy?" The GIs roared with laughter. We were thrilled to have Kaye and his entertainers in our area. We especially liked the young women in the show. Danny was okay, with his stories and jokes, but after all, we knew what American men looked like. June Brunner sang and played her accordion, the only instrument there. She was introduced as "the band." Movie star and singer Monica Lewis also performed, to the troops' delight.

Many of the men wanted to take photographs of the entertainers. I started lining up about ten soldiers at a time, told them to focus their cameras, and when they were ready, I'd say, "Mr. Kaye." He'd turn, smile, and after the cameras clicked, continue his conversation with the colonel. This method meant that all those who wanted photos got them.

For two hours, the men could forget they were soldiers at war. After the show, they returned to the fighting in the hills. Some in that audience never made it back to their homes in the United States. I was lucky. I did.

Far from home, Bob Dolan watched quietly as a scene similar to one he'd seen in his backyard as a child played out on the cold battlefield. At such moments, men had to wonder against whom and why they were fighting.

Some Warmth in the Cold

ROBERT W. DOLAN

During the war, I was a forward observer, someone who watches and reports what the enemy troops are doing. I was involved in brutal combat, including hand-to-hand fighting, and a terrible situation during which I had to order artillery fire on our own position because it was being overrun by the enemy. People ask me how I feel about the Chinese people today after having met them on battlefields as the enemy in Korea. I reply that I have no hatred for them, in part because of an experience I had during a bitterly cold Korean winter.

I was with the Forty-ninth Field Artillery, attached to K Company, Seventeenth Infantry Regiment, Seventh Infantry Division. I was positioned at the front of the American lines, around Kumhwa, where I could observe the Chinese troop movements. The Americans and the Chinese were dug into foxholes, and for several days there was no activity other than the usual skirmishes and sniping that went on.

In 1966, after his second tour of duty in Korea, Bob Dolan came home with Meaghean Ann, his four-year-old adopted daughter.

During the frigid sunny mornings, I watched a young Chinese soldier go out into the open and play with his puppy. They played together in the fire zone, their breath steaming in the cold air. Soldier and pup were totally conspicuous and vulnerable.

The bravery and playfulness of this Chinese soldier impressed me and the other American soldiers so much that no one fired upon him. We encouraged the newest arrivals to our camp to not fire as well. I guess we all felt good when we watched the soldier and the pup. The myth that the Chinese were dog-eaters was dispelled when we saw how kind the soldier was to the puppy. And you know that when you dispel a myth or stereotype about a stranger, it opens up the possibility that other myths and fears about him may also be false. We had something in common with that Chinese soldier, with the people we were fighting in hand-to-hand combat in a war. For those few days, it was the love of a puppy.

Words can have new and unexpected meanings during war,
as Michael Skerik learned.

"Camouflage"

MICHAEL R. SKERIK

I was assigned to the 304th Signal Operations Battalion, Radio Company, and we provided communications for various commands. We landed at Pusan, Korea, in August 1950.

I had been attending a teletype school in Japan for three weeks before the war. In Pusan, with my three weeks' training, I was assigned to a radio teletype team and attached to the Republic of Korea (ROK) I (Eye) Corps.

We pushed off the Pusan Perimeter on my birthday, September 15, 1950, and marched up the east coast of Korea. While we were with the ROKs, we had C rations to eat. We would try to trade the corned beef hash with the Koreans for anything else. But soon the Koreans learned to count the letters in "corned beef hash," and there was no way they would trade with us. We didn't speak Korean, and they didn't speak English, but we both understood.

Some happiness during wartime. In 1951, Mike Skerik and his bride, Bettie, dashed under an archway of silent rifles and a shower of rice.

In Wonsan, as we entered the town, I saw a homemade American flag flying. After our command post was set up, I walked back and, using improvised sign language, talked with the people who owned it. They gave me the flag. It had forty-nine stars—it was made by the Koreans in error before Alaska and Hawaii became states. I kept the flag with me until I received an emergency leave to return to the States. I had to leave some of my things in the supply room when I left Korea, and I never got the flag back.

We left Wonsan after a couple of weeks and moved to Hamhung, a sister city to Hungnam. There we were given 10-in-1 rations. That's food for ten men for one day. The major in charge of the Korean Military Advisory Group teletyped the KMAG headquarters. He told them, "Corned Beef Hash No Good Under Any Condition. Request Necessary Camouflage." A short time later, a small plane landed on the street in front of the command post building. Inside the plane were cases of ketchup and mustard—our "camouflage."

Americans who were fighting in Korea were sent to Japan for R and R. Some, like Jim Landrum, used their spare time away from war to teach English and provide charitable services.

Special Missions

JAMES LANDRUM

After I completed my air force basic training in New York, I joined a group in Denver and we were trained for special intelligence work. I was assigned to a top-secret intelligence B-29 Wing. We reported the information we gathered to a large group of agencies, including the Pentagon, the CIA, and various military commands.

I worked with the Ninety-first Reconnaissance and Ninety-eighth Bomb Wings. We were located at Yokota Air Force Base near Tokyo, Japan. Few of our fellow air force friends knew what we were doing. We were told that if we were ever shot down, the U.S. government would not "know" us or claim we were engaged in intelligence projects. We were given escape routes out of certain Communist countries, as bombers and intelligence aircraft could only fly one way because they didn't hold enough fuel to return. We would have to walk out and meet contacts who would help us.

Working with the Ninety-eighth Bomb Wing, we were always shown their North Korean targets for B-29 night missions. The entire base was responsible for protecting these aircraft against an attack. During one exercise, I remember being in a foxhole on the airfield underneath the planes and looking up from that angle at these huge machines of war.

Our main responsibility was to debrief, or gather information from, the crews of returning spy missions flown near Russia, North Korea, and China. After debriefings, we worked nonstop for seventy-two hours to get the many reports to the military authorities. The mess hall was open twenty-four hours a day because of our working schedule on the base. They served four meals a day, and many times I ate all four of them. My favorite was midnight chow. (The USAF always served good food.)

As part of the psychological warfare, the Ninety-first dropped propaganda leaflets over North Korea to teach them as well as ask for their surrender. This "surrender literature" asked the North Koreans "Why fight?" It told them how to surrender to our military forces in South Korea and explained the benefits of surrendering. We also dropped tinsel—metal foil—from the B-29s. It disrupted the enemy's anti-aircraft weapons on the ground. Early in the war, the enemy's guns fired at the foil instead of the other B-29s that were on bombing missions. Unfortunately, even with

Jim Landrum and one of the jeeps that he used to transport supplies.

Jim Landrum enjoys some baseball during a break from intelligence work.

the tinsel, the North Koreans did hit some of the planes. Thirty-four B-29s were shot down, mostly by Russian Migs, during the Korean War.

When I was off-duty and had time to myself, I taught spoken English at a high school at Kunitachi, in the Tokyo area. My friend John Estep from California and I were the first Americans that the high school staff had ever spoken with. A young man was our interpreter, and he arranged for us to teach a class. To be honest, John and I were so fearful of doing this teaching that we "chickened out" the first day we were to meet with the Japanese students. We got off the train one station before our stop. The next week, we got a good chewing out from the students for not going, and each week after that, we showed up. It was all fun after that first nervous day.

We always had to remove our shoes when we entered the school. On our first day of teaching we were escorted down a long, well-worn, wooden, rather eerie hallway. There was no one around. Finally, we arrived in a room where we met the teaching staff and had tea—you always had to have tea at all meetings. Then we went on to meet our class. The high school students were under extreme pressure to excel and to make good grades in order to go to the best colleges.

John and I were treated with kindness and were greatly appreciated by the students and staff. We visited the students' families and ate with them, even though we were told not to because their food was grown with "honey bucket" fertilizer. We never got sick.

The students constantly asked John and me why the United States had dropped the bombs on them during World War II. They had horrible photographs of Hiroshima and Nagasaki that they seemed to carry with them all the time. We satisfied some of them by explaining the American view, our attempt to end the war, but others kept questioning. Meanwhile, Japanese educators, townspeople, students, and workers assured us that the Japanese people had never wanted the war. The warlords had not listened to the people.

John Allazar from New York City and I also taught weekly at the Hino Orphanage, high in the mountains near Tokyo. The children at this orphanage were mostly African American–Japanese children who had been left behind after the occupation of Japan at the end of World War II. Sadly, they were neglected by both the U.S. and the Japanese governments at the time. To the Japanese, these children were outcasts who would never be accepted in society.

The orphanage was so high in the mountains that there was no road to reach it. We could drive our military jeep part of the way, but we had to stop at the edge of a huge canyon. The only bridge there was not built for vehicles, just pedestrians and bicyclists. The children had only about fifteen cents a day to live on. There was no glass in the windows of the huge old building where they ate. There was a dedicated staff of Japanese people, but conditions were rough.

When we visited, the children would run through the snow to greet us and shake our hands; most of their hands were wrapped in cloth because of infections they had. They greeted us in pain. They didn't have shoes, so we bought them some. Then we bought them clothes. We also brought them sweets and candy from Hino at the

A B-29 assigned to the Ninety-eighth Bomb Wing is parked outside the hangar at Yokota Air Force Base, Japan.

While on leave, many service members took "tourist" snapshots. Jim Landrum's scrapbook includes this photograph of Japanese fisherman near Tokyo. Note their heavy nets and the huge catch in the bins on the left.

bottom of the mountain. Hino was the only town at the time with sidewalks, because it had been bombed during World War II and the Americans had rebuilt it, with sidewalks.

It was so cold in the building where we ate with the children that we decided to buy a wood-burning stove to heat the dining area. We also bought and installed glass in the windows so the snow wouldn't blow in on everyone while they were eating and attending assemblies.

I also worked with our USAF chaplain who had an orphanage in Korea and taught the Bible to Japanese students off the base. Even after I left Japan for the U.S., while I was still in Air Force Intelligence, I spoke to civic and fundraising groups on my days off, and the money collected was sent to the orphanage for food, clothing, building supplies, and health care.

I have never seen anything in the American or Japanese news about this group of neglected children.

James Landrum has continued to work for the benefit of the Korean people since the war.

Family Matters

1952

♦ While peace negotiations continue, so does the fighting. The Battle for Old Baldy is fought in the steaming mountain humidity. In the autumn, troops fight fiercely at the Battle of the Hook. Replacement UN troops are constantly sent to Korea.

♦ In November, there is a presidential election in the United States. Republican candidate Dwight D. Eisenhower is a much-decorated World War II general and appeals to the veterans of that war. He promises that, if elected, he will go to Korea and assess the war.

♦ Voters like what Eisenhower says, and he wins the 1952 presidential election.

♦ On November 29, President-elect Eisenhower secretly flies to Korea and spends three days visiting a Mobile Army Surgical Hospital (MASH) and speaking with South Korean president Syngman Rhee and UN military leaders.

◆ After his return to the United States, Eisenhower says he wants a cease-fire, not a longer war. People become hopeful that the new year will bring an end to the war in Korea.

Louis Lyons's ancestors fought in the Revolutionary War and the Civil War, his brothers fought in World War II, and his nephews were later in the Vietnam War. His parents' strong belief in God sustained them as they watched their sons leave for battle in Korea.

The Cost of War

LOUIS J. LYONS

I grew up in a small town in the coalfields of West Virginia. My daddy was a miner; my mother's father was a Baptist preacher. I was the youngest of nine children.

I enlisted on my seventeenth birthday, even though my mother and father pleaded with me not to. I recall my dad telling me, "Your mom's suffered enough." That's because five of my brothers had served in World War II.

I remember being a youngster and watching my mother sitting and crying, and my dad coming from work and saying, "No mail today." My mother's twin-brother's son was killed on the Bataan Death March in the war, and I saw my mother bewildered, wondering who would be next. [In 1942, the United States and Philippine forces surrendered the Bataan Peninsula in the Philippines to the Japanese. The prisoners of war were forced to march; many died en route.]

Louis J. Lyons

My brother nearest to me in age was in the service and was a mechanic in Korea when the Korean War began. Before six months had passed after my enlistment, I arrived at Chuja-ri in Korea in my unit: C Battery, Seventeenth Field Artillery Battalion. It was February 19, 1951. I was still wet behind the ears and not emotionally prepared to witness what I would see for the next year. I was a cannoneer and, later, a gunner on an eight-inch howitzer. Some of the guns were self-propelled; others were pulled by tractors or trucks. Through June, we moved north as part of the units that formed along "the Kansas Line," the code name for a range of hills just above the 38th parallel, and we roamed back and forth across the line, helping various units. On October 21, our battalion commander, Captain Paul R. Blew, was captured along with his driver by the Chinese forces. The commander was executed on the spot, and his driver was taken prisoner. Of all the events that happened to me while I was in Korea, this single event had the most lasting impact on me. Blew was a man who had served in World War II and was a school principal in Arkansas. He was called back to the military because of the new war. Forty-five days later, he was dead. For forty-nine years, I searched to find out about Captain Blew. I finally located his nephew and heard that the captain's father had died of a heart attack one month after hearing of his son's capture and death.

I thank God for my life every day and know I was fortunate. There were terribly cold winters and unbearably hot summers, complete with chiggers—bugs that made us itchy. I participated in four major engagements and was decorated with four Bronze Stars. We were always very close to the enemy because our job was to fire into their bunkers, to bring the enemy out into the open so our planes could hit them. Floodlights helped us do our job at night. Because of our actions, we were sought by the enemy; they wanted to get rid of us. Maybe they saw the markings "17thFA" on Captain Blew's jeep and that's why he was executed. That's what I suspect. The howitzer I worked on took a direct hit shortly after my departure, and three of the other guys were killed.

My parents were deeply religious people, and when I returned from Korea, they had not heard from me in three months. I called from Denver to tell them I was back in the United States and on my way home. I could hear my mother in the background, praising God.

I learned a number of lessons from the Korean War. I know that children and innocent people suffer. I know that because the United States agreed to the demilitarized zone, our soldiers are still there and still dying. I've learned that it's okay to cry. I try to explain to my grandchildren that there are no winners in war and that we must learn to live in harmony in this world.

Louis J. Lyons passed away shortly after sending his story to be included in this book.

Our huge world seemed like a very small place when the two Charlesworth brothers served in Korea. Eventually, they found themselves enjoying a few hours of food and fun together.

A Brother's Love

ROBERT D. CHARLESWORTH

Don and I were two of six children (four boys, all of whom served in various branches of the service at various times, and two girls). We were raised in Buffalo, New York. When the Korean War broke out in 1950, we knew it would eventually affect us. We were both recent high school graduates. Neither of us wished to wait for the draft, so we decided to enlist.

Don went into the army in February 1951 and arrived in Korea in July. My father begged me to hold off because my mother was deeply troubled about her sons going off to war. I waited until October 1951, when I enlisted in the air force. I was nineteen years old.

I was with a headquarters unit of the Fifth Air Force. My duties as Military Police ranged from security details and town patrol to chasing prisoners (our own), and honor guard formations. Don's unit was a heavy mortar company, the Thirty-eighth

Regimental Combat Team, Second Infantry Division. In September 1951, just a month before I enlisted, Don's unit was under heavy fire at the Battle of Bloody Ridge. He suffered shrapnel wounds on his left side from his legs to his head and was sent to the 8209th MASH, where he was hospitalized. The medics did a fine job of cleaning the shrapnel out, but some damage was sustained. He lost some mobility in his fingers, and the vision in his left eye was impaired to about thirty percent.

We wrote to each other during my air force boot training and, later, my police training. When I completed the training, I let Don know that I was coming to Korea. He was furious that I had volunteered to serve there, but I simply told him to keep looking over his shoulder, because one day I'd be there.

When I arrived in Seoul in April 1952, I waited a bit and then asked my first sergeant for permission to visit my brother before he was sent home. I had learned through his letters that his unit had been relieved from the MLR (Main Line of Resistance) and sent to Koje-do Island. Don had been hospitalized there because of a serious jaw infection.

Bob (left) and Don Charlesworth—truly brothers in arms.

Within a week, the sergeant told me that three days of temporary leave had been approved. I was advised to carry a sidearm, since danger spots were known to exist en route. On May 26, 1952, at seven o'clock in the evening, I boarded the EUSAK (Eighth U.S. Army in Korea) Express train at the Seoul Railroad Transportation Office for the trip to Pusan. I carried my bag and wore a pistol on my belt.

The overnight ride to Pusan was both tiring and exciting. Sleep was almost impossible in the coach-type seats, and for security reasons the cars were in total darkness. For some of the night, I lay on the floor because the train was struck by rocks and stones, or perhaps gunfire. We had been advised that some guerrilla activity against the train was normal.

The train arrived in Pusan the following morning at about seven o'clock. When I arrived, I was not aware of the location of the ferry to Koje-do Island or the length of time the trip would take. I ate breakfast in a nearby mess hall and then asked about the ferry. I learned that the ferry was a fairly big ship and that it made only one trip each day to the island. It left at 7:45 A.M. and returned to Pusan at about 4:30 in the afternoon. The trip was four hours long, one way. The ferry dock was just a stone's throw from the train station.

By this time, I had missed the ferry for the day. I checked with the army units, the Red Cross, even with the chaplain for the entire Pusan area to find help in getting to the island that day. Nothing could be done. Even if I had made the ferry, I would not have been allowed on because I had not been cleared as a passenger. That had to be done a day before your trip, but I didn't know that. I was very dejected.

The chaplain told me that the only way I could get to the island that day was for him to rent a boat and take me there, but he couldn't. He cautioned me not to try such a venture on my own, because Korean thugs would agree to take me, for a price, and then once we were out to sea, they would probably take all my possessions and dump me overboard.

So I spent the day in Pusan where, much to my surprise, I met the military police. A sergeant demanded to know why I was carrying a loaded weapon in Pusan. He said that I was in violation of a no-weapons zone. I explained why I had the gun. I produced my identification and my orders. Finally, the officer said he did not wish to ruin my visit with my brother. He ordered me to remove the weapon and put it in my bag, which I did. He warned me that if I was seen wearing the gun in Pusan, I would be arrested. I thanked the officer endlessly.

Later that day, I went to be cleared as a passenger on the next day's ferry to the island. Early the next morning, I boarded the ferry. The weather was clear and the spring sun was warm. The trip was uneventful, and I was standing on the Koje-do landing at about noon.

When I disembarked, I asked for directions to the Thirty-eighth Infantry Regiment. There was no vehicle traffic heading in that direction, so I began to walk. I must have walked for several miles on the dirt roads, through a series of curves and hills, when I finally came to a tented unit and spotted a sign—IMPEL BLACK, 38TH INFANTRY REGIMENT.

I spoke to a company clerk. He went to his locater file and announced that my brother Don was in the unit. I laughed and said, "I know he is. Where is he?" He gave me directions, and when I arrived at another tented area, I asked for Don by name. Several men told me he was in the chow hall.

I nervously headed in that direction, and when I entered, I saw two men working. I asked for Don. One of the men looked me over and asked, "Are you his brother?" I answered I was, and he got excited. "He said you were coming," he said. "He's in the latrine. Stay here and I'll get him." The man ran out the door, and the other man asked if I'd eaten anything. When I said I hadn't, he fixed a quick tray of food for me. I was too excited to eat, but I tried.

Suddenly, the door flew open and Don burst in. "Hey, Walyo!" he shouted. (That's a term from our neighborhood.) We hugged, punched each other, and shouted. The other two men stood there grinning from ear to ear. Don and I kept clowning around like school kids.

When we finally calmed down, he told me he was shaving when his buddy came in and asked, "Didn't you tell me your brother might come to visit?" Don said yes. His friend replied, "Well, he's in the chow hall." Don said he almost cut his throat when he heard the news.

We left the chow hall and went to the tents, where a spare bunk was found for me. The events of the day and the men I met are somewhat blurred now, but I recall that Don and I managed to find a jeep and toured some parts of the island. The compounds that housed the POWs were closely guarded by mounted guns in the surrounding hills. These guns were reminders of earlier trouble on the island, when Chinese prisoners rioted and managed to capture U.S. Army Brigadier Francis T.

Dodd as a hostage. The island was still under martial law, and enforcement measures were strict.

I had brought a camera and film with me, so many pictures of our reunion were taken that day. As the day wound down, I met several officers in the unit. When Don and I went to mess that evening, one of the officers approached us and invited us to join the officers for dinner in their mess, a smaller, private room off the main hall. The officers gathered there were very gracious, and they made room at their table for us. It was a gesture I have never forgotten.

That evening, before partying with the troops, Don and I wrote separate letters home and put them in one envelope for mailing. In what can only be described as a chance event, our reunion date, May 28, 1952, was our parents' twenty-fifth wedding anniversary.

That evening also produced a story I've never forgotten. Don recounted the terror-filled night of his arrival in Korea the previous July. All the replacements—the soldiers—were jammed onto a train and taken north to a point where convoy trucks were waiting. They went from train to truck and continued north to a drop-off spot. From there they went on foot to join their companies. Enemy mortar fire was constant that night, so when Don finally reached his unit, he was shoved into a bunker.

A platoon leader told him to get some sleep, that a patrol would be formed when the mortar attack stopped. When the attack ended, Don was ordered out on his first patrol. Don's recollection was that his fear was so overwhelming he could barely move. He said he was looked after by some older squad members.

It was time for me to go the next morning. Somewhat in a daze, I gathered my gear together and said goodbye to some new friends. The ferry was due to leave at 12:30 P.M. Once again, a jeep and driver were available, so Don and I were driven to the ferry landing. I checked in with the loading officer and logged on the passenger manifest, or list.

We had to wait a bit, so Don and I stood and made our goodbyes. Don finally said he had to report for duty, and the jeep was on short notice and had to be returned. I understood, and we said our final goodbye. He drove away from the landing, waving, and I watched the jeep move along that dirt road. Don continued to wave as the jeep wound its way around the hills and disappeared from view.

In June, one month after our meeting, Don was sent back to the United States to finish his service time at Camp Kilmer in New Jersey. In the spring of 1953, he was taken ill and transferred to an army hospital in Pennsylvania. He died there, on November 12, 1953, at the age of twenty-three. He was buried with military honors four days later near Buffalo, New York.

At his funeral mass, I was plagued with the vision of our Koje-do farewell. I could see the jeep disappearing into the hills and Don waving.

Many veterans recall the thousands of Korean children they met during their years overseas and still have photographs of the hungry and ragged tots who tugged at their uniforms and their hearts. Chong Suk Dickman was one of those children.

Thank You

CHONG SUK DICKMAN

In 1952, I was a seven-year-old Korean girl who did not see much of the direct war and conflict in my country. I did, however, know that all the males—fathers and brothers—in our village were gone to help in the war. I lived in a little farming village that was surrounded by mountains and filled with beautiful flowers in the spring. The village has not changed much since then and would be missed traveling south from Seoul, except for a little sign that reads OKSAN.

Children are the same no matter how big their town or which country they live in. We were fearful, yet we played, dreamed, and hoped. We did not know why our country was at war, who the players were, or what this event would mean in history. We just knew that our dads were gone and we were hungry. During the day, we went to school and helped our mothers. At night, we would seek protection in bunkers or foxholes. My first contact with Americans came in the form of fliers dropped from planes. The fliers read, "You are safe. We are here."

I did not know about America or the United States, but I had heard of "Yankees" and how they were here to save us. One morning, a few children ran through the village yelling, "Yankees are here!" Like most kids, who let curiosity drive them, I ran with the others to the top of a hill and saw two men standing next to an

Many veterans of the Korean War were touched by the large numbers of children they saw in the city streets and villages of Korea. These children lived in Pusan.

open vehicle. Years later, I recognized their vehicle as a jeep. These men seemed enormous. My head lifted as if I were scanning a mountain, and my mouth opened with awe at how dirty the Yankees were. All I could tell my mother was that "Yankees are very dirty."

Looking back, I do not know if the soldiers were African American or if they were wearing camouflage on their faces. If you can imagine seeing a person for the first time and not understanding that they could be of different size and color—that is what I experienced. The soldiers must have been surveying the land. After they spoke to each other, they left our small part of the world. I have imagined that they said that ours was a peaceful village.

The next most memorable experience I had with the U.S.A. had to do with food. In America, many people are fortunate not to have to know what true hunger is. When I was young, like most of my country's people, I felt the pangs and numbness of hunger. One morning when I went to school, our teacher told us that food had been delivered by American soldiers. I never learned how the food got to our village or to our school. The barrels were large enough to fit three of my classmates inside. I still remember the stamp on the top of the drums, the first English letters I ever saw: U.S.A.

We were all hoping for rice or barley, and we drooled at the thought of so much food. When the barrels were opened, we found that we had an endless supply of powdered milk. Our diets had not consisted of dairy products at all, but we drank until our bellies were satisfied. We even made the milk into thick pancakes that we all devoured at lunch. This foreign aid, being foreign to our systems, caused all who drank it to suffer for days with diarrhea. Though our bodies were purged of all that we had, we were grateful.

I write this memory now, as a U.S. citizen for over thirty years, to thank all the men who served in Korea. You changed our lives. We did not know who you were, where the United States was, or why you had to be there. We only knew you as our guardian angels.

I married a Yankee soldier who served for over twenty years. We have a son and a son-in-law who serve in the armed forces. Help given during war does make sense, and it does make a difference. Take it from one who knows.

Far from home, soldiers like Gunther Dohse saw firsthand what family life was like in the villages of Korea. Amid the horror of war, he watched as a ramshackle machine brought momentary joy to the children — and him.

A Puff of Rice

GUNTHER DOHSE

On the morning of November 29, 1950, after surviving the first Chinese onslaught at Yudam-ni, deep in the Chosin Reservoir, we were ordered to drop all of our personal belongings in a pile. Those who were reluctant were assured that the supply people would load them up and take them away for us. Lighten your load, marine. There is tough walking ahead.

We weren't gone more than a couple of hundred yards when one man in the column said, "Look back." The pile of belongings was in flames. I had no interest thereafter in carrying personal belongings.

I don't know how many of us believed that we would fight again. We were the marines of Charlie Company of the Fifth Marine Regiment, the same regiment that distinguished itself at Belleau Wood in France during World War I. A month before, we had escaped the bitter cold and the encirclement of our unit by Chinese soldiers

Gunther Dohse enjoys the sunshine at San Francisco Bay. A week later, on June 24, 1950, he was aboard the USNS General Edwin D. Patrick as the Korean War began.

at the Chosin Reservoir in North Korea. Our losses were great. We regrouped at Masan, at the southern tip of South Korea. With new replacements, new equipment, and more training, we were ready to return to action in record time.

It was January 29, 1951, and I was nineteen years old. My unit was alerted to come to the aid of the people of the village of Chachon-Dong. Our leaders told us that guerrillas were about to attack the village and deprive the people of their food.

We left our camp late in the evening, after dark, and made a forced march of about twelve miles. We carried heavy loads, often exceeding sixty pounds. We arrived at Chachon-Dong shortly after midnight. I was exhausted. We were quickly assigned to villagers' homes to sleep.

The home where I was to stay was an L-shaped hut with a straw-thatched roof. It was on a path that ran along a stream. The hut was the home of a family with several young children, including a couple of curious boys. There was an older gentleman with a high black hat, an old woman, a young woman who was nursing a baby, and others. But the person I remember most fondly was a handicapped girl who did most of the work. She was the one who, dragging her lame foot, was the first person up each morning. At dawn, I saw her misshapened back as she stooped to stoke the fire. She was the one who fetched the heavy pails of water to cook the "sticky rice" and brew the tea.

This was my first time in the home of a South Korean family. Even though it was icy cold outside, the hut was cozy and warm, especially the floor. The clay floor was heated by hot air that passed through tubes beneath the floor. It was the hardworking girl who went outside to keep the fire smoldering in a chamber that vented into the heating system. Three other marines and I occupied the smaller room of the hut, while the family lived in the larger wing.

My fighting position was behind a low stone wall that surrounded the compound of the house. On the other side of the wall was a path, and below the path was the stream. I had an easy position to defend. Any enemy approaching my position had to cross a creek edged with brittle ice, then climb up a small bank. The enemy would have been silhouetted against the sky. Had an enemy come, it would have been like target practice at the firing range.

My first night at watch was clear and cold. When I approached my post the second night, I found someone had placed a chair near the wall. On the chair I found a few pieces of rice-taffy candy.

We kept watch for several nights and hid during the daylight hours, but soon it was apparent that the guerrillas knew we were in the village, protecting the people. Finally, we were allowed to come out of the huts during the day.

What a sight!

For the first time, I was able to see beyond the stone wall where I had taken my turns at watch. The path in front of my wall emptied into the village square. A school at one side of the square had become a battalion field kitchen, set up to feed us. The

Many veterans' scrapbooks have one of these amusing certificates, which they received as souvenirs when they crossed the 180th meridian.

Two papa-sans take an afternoon walk in Pusan.

other huts along the path were similar in size and shape to the one I was sleeping in. In the yard of the last home on the path, a "papa-san" (grandfather) labored over a homemade contraption. He was dressed in his finest pants and jacket and wore a stovepipe hat. His strange machine was a metal drum with a door attached to one end. The door was locked securely with a substantial lever. A prominently mounted pressure gauge was visible from a distance.

The angle of this contraption made me think it was a cannon used by circus folks to shoot an acrobat into a net. A fire under the drum sent the needle on the gauge quivering and a host of children into happy anticipation. As the crucial moment known only to the papa-san arrived, the elder shouted a warning that caused the children to cover their ears.

As the children screeched, the old man activated the lever. The door flew open with a bang. In a cloud of steam, puffed rice rained over the young audience. A happy feeding frenzy ensued. Then the puffed-rice shooter was reloaded, and the spectacle was repeated several more times for the delighted children.

For the first time since I'd arrived in Korea, I understood why I was there. The vision of the children of Chachon-Dong kept me going through ten more months of war. *Semper fidelis.*

The events of September 11, 2001, brought Gunther Dohse more Korean War memories
He shared them in a letter to a friend:

You remember the buddies we dragged in shelter halves and ponchos off the hills in Korea and didn't care whether it was green side or brown side out? We didn't have the time to be grateful that it wasn't us. There was no time to mourn the loss.

I don't really know when losses didn't matter anymore. . . . I think it was about the time when I helped drag Chic Sorenson part of the day and half of the night along the side of a mountain pass coming out of Yudam-ni the first day of December in 1950. It was the day I fired my weapon without thinking and making eye contact with the Chinese soldier cowering in a snow cave along the trail. I'd like to forget that day, but I can't. It was a starless night when we dumped Chic in the snow, covered him with branches, and listened to the words of the skipper but didn't hear them. It was a relief to be rid of the load, to have a chance to escape, but I am ashamed to this day of not having brought him home.

It took nearly fifty years—and pure coincidence—for Vincent Krepps to learn what happened to his brother, Richard. Many families are still waiting to hear about their lost ones.

One Twin Came Home

VINCENT A. KREPPS

My twin brother, Richard, and I grew up in Pennsylvania with our three sisters. In 1949, after we graduated from high school, we and three of our childhood friends joined the army. After our basic training, my brother and I were both assigned the Second Infantry Division, Eighty-second AAA Battalion. Richard was a cannoneer and I was a tank driver in the same battery. Our three friends were assigned elsewhere.

We arrived in Korea in August 1950. Just thirteen days after getting there, I was near the Naktong River, guarding against a North Korean attack. My tank was hit, and we abandoned it. The night seemed to go on forever. Our troops were surrounded. The North Korean troops were advancing, and they seemed to cover the hillsides like ants.

Eventually, I was taking cover in a ditch and I had no weapon except one hand grenade. There was a call for a tank driver. At first I didn't reply, but finally I answered that I could move the abandoned tank that was blocking our way. Under heavy enemy fire, I had to make emergency repairs on the vehicle and then drive it through the enemy roadblock. I kept driving for miles, with my grenade in my lap, until I reached American troops. They rushed to help our unit, but when they returned, the news was bad—most of my unit had been killed or taken prisoner.

A week later, I was back with what was left of my unit. My brother, Richard, had experienced his first taste of war, too. We had only been in Korea for three weeks. When we spent time together, Richard and I talked about home, our dad's new car, and our future. Soon, Richard was called back to the front. On September 4, 1950, we hugged and said goodbye for what would be the last time.

In 1950, Vince (left) and Dickie are in uniform.

Curly-haired twins Vincent (left) and Richard Krepps pose for a baby picture.

Within a week, Richard was wounded in battle. Soldiers used to say that if you had a wound bad enough to get you sent home, instead of to the hospital ship or to a hospital in Japan, you had a "million-dollar wound." Richard's injury wasn't bad enough. A month after he was wounded, I was injured and on my way to the same hospital Richard had been sent to. A nurse said I'd just missed him; Richard had recovered and been sent back to war.

During the first week of December 1950, I rejoined my unit. Near Kunu-ri, the UN troops were overwhelmed by the Chinese Communists, and many troops were killed or taken as prisoners-of-war. My brother, Richard Krepps, was officially declared missing-in-action as of December 1, 1950.

There was no news of Richard's whereabouts. We had Richard's letters at home in Pennsylvania, but his last letter was sent to our sister Loretta in October 1950. Then, in the spring of 1951, someone in our family saw a picture of Richard in a local newspaper. It was a propaganda photograph that had been released by the Chinese Communists. It showed eleven American POWs lined up at a prison camp "somewhere in Korea." Richard was in the front row, and he didn't look well.

By the middle of 1951, I was home from the war, but I continued serving in the

The Krepps family recognized Dickie at the far left of this newspaper photograph of POWs.

army throughout its duration. We kept hoping that Richard was alive, that he was being taken care of by his captors. We waited two years, until the war ended, for word of Richard. Still we heard nothing.

In January 1954, our family received a letter from the Department of the Army saying that the Chinese Communists had unofficially listed Richard as having died June 21, 1951, at Camp 5, at Pyoktong, North Korea, near the Yalu River. The cause of death was listed as pellagra, a disease caused by vitamin deficiency. Richard had turned twenty years old just one month before his death.

Like other veterans of the Korean War, I got on with my life. I pursued a career in drafting. But from the time we got the notification of Richard's death, I tried to learn more about his last days, find where he is buried, and bring him home. I interviewed former POWs of the Second Division, hoping they'd have some information. No luck.

Then, in December 1998, I received a letter from a veteran named Ronald D. Lovejoy, who lives in Nevada. His daughter had seen one of my notes about my search on the Internet. She mentioned it to her father, and he wrote to me. The date on his letter was December 1, 1998, exactly forty-eight years to the day that Richard was captured at Kunu-ri, North Korea. I held on to Ronald's letter for three months before I could call him. I feared that he would be like other POWs I'd spoken with, that he had only been in the same camp and didn't known much of my brother. I was wrong.

Ronald had been a POW in the same hospital where my brother died. The hospital was an old Japanese temple located at Camp 5. Ronald was very ill, and Richard had been put beside him on the floor of the hospital. They talked about going home, their families, and food. Richard was very sick and very weak; he could not walk. The only medicine the prisoners were given was charcoal. He refused to eat the barley and millet mush that was given to them. One morning, Ronald turned to speak to Richard, and there was no answer. Like many prisoners, Richard was so sick he gave up.

Ronald told me that the guards took Richard outside and stacked him like cordwood on the pile of other dead POWs until the burial team came to pick them up. Ronald had my brother's wallet for a while, but he lost it somewhere at the hospital.

Ronald remained at the camp until a month after the war ended and didn't arrive back in the United States until late August 1953.

I finally met Ronald at a POW reunion in July 1999. He gave me a photo from Richard's wallet, a picture Ronald had carried with him for all those years. The photograph was a full-length shot in which Richard was holding a cane. It was the same picture he'd sent home during his brief stay in the Japanese hospital, the time when I arrived just after he'd left. The picture he sent home only showed the upper part of his body and his face; I think he cut away the rest of the picture so our family wouldn't see the cane and worry more about him.

The damaged but cherished photograph that Vince Krepps waited forty-eight years to receive.

I am now more at peace than ever before. I know that Richard had someone to talk to, someone who tried to help him, someone who was his last friend, someone who could be like a family member and care for him. Still, I wait for the day when we can bring Richard home.

Vincent Krepps was awarded the Silver Star for valor for running the roadblock in hopes of saving his unit.

Many teenaged boys volunteered for service in the Korean War, just as teenaged boys had during past wars. Fred Cox discovered that there were two groups of kids in Korea—those who had been born there and those who went there to fight. As he notes, many of the service members lost "a big chunk of our youth" and innocence during the war.

The "Kids" of the Korean War

FRED L. COX

Korean children may have been the most prepared of any youngsters to survive a war. Their country had gone through years of occupation by the Japanese, and throughout history, Korea had been invaded many times before. They were survivors. They used their wit, charm, and a great deal of persistence to find food, shelter, safety, and clothing. They learned very quickly how to perform jobs for us kids in uniform.

One important point about the hordes of little Korean children—I never saw or heard of any thieving by these huge bunches of kids. They were a credit to their country. The kids of Korea were burdened with a heavy load during the war, but it didn't take the kids in uniform long to show them that it was okay to be children, to have fun, and to smile.

I turned twenty on my way to Korea. I was naive, innocent (read: dumb),

Fred Cox poses with local girls in traditional Korean dresses.

inexperienced, and scared. I joined the army after high school so I could learn a trade; I joined the Signal Corps, and spent fourteen months training in New Jersey. Then the war broke out. I had not yet learned to think and act like a man, but I wasn't much different from most of the other guys with me.

I was not a combat soldier. The army had spent a lot training us for the signal work and didn't want us out fighting. We usually found ourselves just behind the fighting, where it was a little safer; I never shot at anyone, but I was shot at plenty! I was a member of the Fifty-first Signal Battalion, T & T Company Carrier Platoon, assigned to I Corps. I was trained to provide plain old telephone service on cable, open wire, or VHF radio. I served with several units; my last was with the Ninth Republic of Korea Division. We were moved individually, so I didn't stay with the same team for very long.

For the Korean children, our biggest attraction was our food. At first, they couldn't speak English, but after only a few days they knew how to ask for jobs, cuss a little bit, and ask for handouts. On the run to the north, we didn't see very many civilians up close; they were all escaping to the south, carrying everything they had. In the extreme north of Korea, we saw only people in uniforms, no children at all.

On the big rush for the south, in retreat, we once again met the civilians and the Korean soldiers who were trying to save themselves. There wasn't much time for socializing then, just begging because conditions were so bad. Whenever and wherever we set up a communications center for a day or more, we began to find kids underfoot. We'd give them cigarettes and Hershey's chocolate bars, which we believe they traded for food. Often, we let some of the children eat our food.

For a while, we were camped on the Pak-han River, just west of the city of Chunchon, in central Korea. The beach on the river was of sand and mica and provided the GIs and the village kids with a beautiful swimming hole for the summer of

1950. Soldiers and kids swam in the nude, without any embarrassment. Close by, the children's mothers washed clothes on the huge rocks near the edge of the river. For a small fee, they also washed the soldiers' clothing.

Usually one of the teenagers would try to get a job as a houseboy, doing just about anything to stay with us and have some degree of safety. But food was what the kids wanted most. The little ones would come to the garbage cans just outside of our mess tent and take food from the cans. When I first saw this, I was revolted and I tried to chase the children away. Some of the other guys explained to me that the kids were

This scene of hungry Korean children rummaging through the army garbage cans . . .

. . . led to soldiers like Fred Cox sharing their rations with them as often as possible.

89

Fred Cox's pockets are bulging with food.

hungry and were getting food for themselves and their families. It just didn't seem right that kids should have to scrape out garbage cans. But what else could they do? All of us began to take more than we could eat so we could give the excess to the children. The cooks often prepared more than they knew we would eat, just so there would be plenty of leftovers for the children. Sometimes, the cooks made extra rice to repay the villagers for jobs they did for us.

There's a photo of me while I was with the First Cavalry. My jacket pockets are bulging. (Looks like I didn't know how to match my buttons and buttonholes, either!) I had learned that we would not always be where we could eat hot food in a mess tent, so I carried Hershey's chocolate bars and packaged food from C rations in my pockets.

Chocolate bars! Oh, how we hated them! We were swamped with them, so we gladly gave them away. I tried eating one after the war. I failed.

Soldiers like Bob Charlesworth helped Korean boys earn a bit to help their families stay alive while war was waged in the countryside. Most veterans can recall the houseboys who worked for coins, chocolate bars, rations, and even small-sized, worn-out soldiers' uniforms.

The Incomparable Skosh

ROBERT D. CHARLESWORTH

I n 1952, while the city of Seoul was recovering, one or two local banks in the downtown area opened for business. One of their customers was our industrious houseboy, whom we called Skosh.

Lee Jung Nai, or Skosh, was a delightful teenaged youngster who labored in our Quonset hut after school in an effort to keep thirty or more GIs clean-shaven, well-polished, and upright. For his efforts, he was paid each month on our payday. He was smart enough to get his pay before our card games, and betting, began.

It fell to some of us to counsel Skosh to save his money and to open a bank account. He did so, and we regularly checked his bank passbook to monitor his deposits.

"Bedcheck Charlie" was an infrequent night visitor to the Seoul area. Charlie was a North Korean who flew a small-engine fixed-wing plane under radar where he couldn't be located and stopped. Whenever Charlie came, he dropped a few grenades to damage and disrupt whatever he could. Then he disappeared, only to return another night.

On one of Charlie's visits, our unit got into the nearby trenches for cover. Skosh was sleeping over in a spare bunk this one night. When Charlie finally left, and we returned to our bunks, Skosh was missing. A brief search failed to locate him. We assumed he had run to his home.

Bob Charlesworth with Skosh.

This houseboy earns money washing soldiers' clothing. He cleans the dirty clothes by rubbing them against the rocks and then rinsing them in the river.

One of the houseboys was Moon. His duties included cleaning the living area of the soldiers' barracks, making beds, and caring for rifles. Like many houseboys, he wore some of the soldiers' spare clothing.

Some hours later, when we were all bedded down, the door of the hut opened and then slammed shut. We heard heavy breathing. Flashlights scanned the hut, and we found Skosh on the floor, huffing and puffing. After he was calm, he told us in his unique broken English that he had run to the bank to make sure his money was safe. The hut erupted with laughter. Skosh was furious with us and wouldn't talk to us for days.

Some time later, after bits of conversation with him, we learned that on that night he had feared the North Koreans were coming again, and so he ran to secure his money. We then understood that his work for us, and our payment to him, was in fact his security for his future and perhaps that of his family.

Our "little" Korean teenager was really a very mature man.

Born in a small town in Maine during the Great Depression, Paul Tardiff thought he knew what hunger was, but what he saw in Korea was more severe than he ever imagined. The army's garbage was as valuable as gold, and for some, it was a treasure worth digging for in the night.

While Soldiers Sleep

PAUL E. TARDIFF

There's a lot of suffering caused by war. Not just the pain and anguish that combat soldiers experience but also the horror brought to innocent civilians. I was a combat soldier in Korea, a corporal assigned to I Company, Seventh Infantry Regiment, Third Infantry Division from April to November 1952. I fought, was wounded, and was evacuated. While I will never forget the gallant men I served with, I will also never forget the heartbreaking scenes I came upon, where civilians were paying the price for the manmade chaos and destruction of their country.

In July 1952, we were in the Chorwon Valley, moving north under darkness. All around we could hear heavy artillery and gunfire. When we finally got the word that we were going to bivouac for the night, we were near exhaustion. Our rear headquarters realized that we needed a morale boost, so they sent trucks loaded with chow, or food, to the area.

Paul Tardiff

The food was served from thermal cans that kept it hot. Each soldier went through the chow line holding his mess kit, an aluminum pan-like dish with a cover, locked together with a metal bar. (When you opened the kit, the metal bar became a handle.)

Each of us received a generous portion of instant mashed potatoes, stewed beef, and vegetables. After leaving the chow line, we found a spot to sit and enjoy our food. When we finished eating, we emptied our leftovers into a large pit that had been dug for that purpose. After all the garbage was in the pit, the hole was filled in.

Guards were in place, and the rest of us pitched our pup tents—small tents big enough to hold two sleeping soldiers. (Each soldier carried half a tent in his backpack.) It was not long before most of us were asleep. About an hour later, the guards' voices woke me. I crawled out of my sleeping bag and stuck my head out of the tent. I asked what was going on. A guard told me, "Come take a look."

A small group of Korean women, some with tiny babies tied to their backs or very small children clinging to their sides, were digging our garbage out of the hole—and eating it. For their safety, the guards made them leave. I crawled back into the tent, but I could not sleep.

The next day, we were told that we would spend yet another night in the area and, again, we would have hot chow. Our unit had Republic of Korea (ROK) soldiers attached to it. I was a squad leader, and Kim Dong Soon, one of the ROK soldiers, was assigned to me. He spoke pretty good English. I asked him to see if he could locate the women and children who had visited our garbage pit during the night. If so, I asked him to tell them to come to our camp around four o'clock that afternoon.

By this time, everyone in our company knew of the women and their babies. At four o'clock, the trucks carrying the thermal cans with our hot food arrived. The chow line was set up, and the soldiers got out their mess kits and filed through. As

In the war, villages and cities like Seoul were destroyed. The ruins were often replaced with new buildings, but some villages simply "disappeared," never to be rebuilt.

the soldiers searched for places to sit and eat, they could not help but notice the small group of women watching with their babies and small children.

I walked to one of the mothers who had a baby on her back and placed my mess kit in her hands. Kim Dong Soon told her it was a gift, and that she should take it. She did, and she began to eat. One by one, other soldiers followed me, until each one of the women and children had food to eat. They spoke to us in Korean, each expressing thanks.

We were gone the next day, but the memories of those displaced war refugees haunt me to this day.

On Memorial Day 2002, Command Sergeant Major Paul E. Tardiff, U.S. Army (Retired), was awarded the Silver Star for action that had taken place in Korea fifty years earlier.

After the War

1953

◆ The UN armies continue the pattern of limited advances and retreats. Soviet leader Joseph Stalin dies in March.

◆ During "Operation Little Switch" in April, some of the prisoners are returned to their Communist or UN forces. Hundreds of Chinese and nearly five thousand Koreans are sent north. Hundreds of Korean and non-Korean soldiers are sent back to the south. The exchange is made at Panmunjom.

◆ Leaders continue with peace talks, but little progress is made. Thousands more troops and civilians die.

◆ The Battle of Pork Chop Hill drags on from April until July. Ninety-six American soldiers are trapped on the hill. The Chinese forces constantly attack the pinned-down men. Soon there are only fifty-five soldiers left. Still they fight. Reinforcements arrive, and the fighting continues. By the last days of the battle there are five battalions of Americans defending the hill. On July 10, after such great loss of life in its defense, the hill is evacuated.

- By the end of July, the last UN ground fighting has taken place. Nearly half a million UN troops have been killed and another half a million are wounded or missing.

- In Panmunjom at 1000 (10 A.M.) on July 27, 1953, Lieutenant General William Harrison, the lead UN negotiator, and North Korean General Nam Il, senior delegate for the Communists, sign the armistice that officially ends the fighting. No representative of the Republic of Korea (ROK) attends because of ROK unhappiness with the agreement. General Mark Clark, the commander of the UN forces, also signs the cease-fire document. This ends the war at 2200 (10 P.M.) that day but does nor bring permanent peace between North Korea and South Korea. A formal peace treaty is never signed.

- No one knows exactly how many civilians were killed during the war. It is estimated that more than three million people died in Korea between June 25, 1950, and July 27, 1953.

The cramped quarters of a tank, a former German soldier from World War II, and a familiar face from long ago are some of Ernie Romans's memories of Korea.

A Blast of Luck

ERNIE ROMANS

For more than one hundred years, members of my family have served in the military during wartime. My grandfather from Cape Breton served in both the Boer War and World War I. My father served in the Canadian navy during World War II; one of his brothers served in the army; and Dave, his youngest brother, flew with the Royal Air Force. Uncle Dave, only twenty-one years old, and his flying crew were shot down over Norway in 1941. He is a war hero, and Romans Avenue in Halifax, Nova Scotia, is named after him.

I joined the Canadian army in October 1951, when I was seventeen. I was in the Reserve Army (Armoured Corps) Halifax Rifles and was posted to Petawawa, Ontario. There, I became a member of D Squadron, Royal Canadian Dragoons Armoured Corps. I was a wireless radio operator and gunner in a tank. We were trained on Sherman tanks from World War II and later on British Centurion tanks.

There were a lot of guns on a tank: a 76-mm, a 50-caliber mounted on the turret, and two 30-caliber guns.

I was scheduled to go to Germany but was turned down because I was not married, and only married men were being sent to replace other married men who had spent eighteen months there. After I found out I wasn't going to Germany, I broke rules, got into trouble, and was sent on charge—marched in front of my commanding officer to hear my charge. I was to be sentenced to detention or confined to the barracks. My squadron commander was very upset and informed me that D Squadron was going to Korea but he would not let me go because I "might shoot one of [my] own people!" I got flip and said, "Yes, sir!" I was transferred to squadron headquarters. Soon I was down on my knees scrubbing and waxing the floors.

I complained that I hadn't joined the army to stay in Canada. I said I could have done that as a civilian, and if the army didn't get me out of the country, I was going to take off. A second lieutenant was standing behind me and said he'd heard me complaining. He could send me to detention for ninety days for what I'd said. Luckily for me, the lieutenant had been in the Halifax Rifles with me long before, and he didn't send me to detention.

A short time later, we were on pay parade (that's when we lined up every two weeks to receive our pay from the paymaster), and a man arrived and called out some names. Those called, about fifteen of us, were to report to the colonel's office immediately. The colonel went down the line and asked each man if he wanted to go to Korea. Of course, my answer was yes. We were eventually put on a troop train headed across the country to Vancouver, British Columbia. Then we took a bus to Seattle, Washington. A few days later, we were on an American troop ship—there were 5000 American troops and 500 Canadians on board.

The voyage to Japan took about seventeen days, and when we arrived, we were sent to a camp in Hiro for a few days. Then it was on to Korea. I was posted to the Lord Strathcona's Horse (Royal Canadians) A Squadron. It was October 1953, just a month before my twenty-first birthday. I landed in Korea after the cease-fire.

When I arrived, the LdSH were on exercises, and their tanks were on the side of a hill. All the tanks in the squadron had names that began with A—mine was

In 1954, Canada's prime minister, Louis St. Laurent, visited Korea. Servicemen performed a "drive past" of tanks in honor of the visit.

called "Analyses." When the exercises were over, I was introduced to my fellow crew members. A tank crew usually consists of a driver, a co-driver, a wireless operator/gunner (me), and a crew commander/loader.

My driver's name was John S. He took care of the tank as if it were his personal vehicle, and he kept the engine running in top condition. The engine compartment was so clean you could have eaten out of it.

One day, I saw John looking at some photographs, and I asked to look at them. One photo showed John in a German uniform with sergeant's stripes on the sleeve. He was also wearing an Iron Cross around his neck. I said, "You were a Nazi. How many Canadians did you kill during World War II?" John replied that he had not been a Nazi; he was an Austrian who was forced into the German army. I was surprised to learn this about him.

In January 1954, John went to Japan for some R and R. Around January 18, our commanding officer informed us that we were going behind American lines for gunnery practice. I told the officer that we didn't have a driver. He said he would get us one. The next morning, I woke up very early and wrote a letter to my mother telling her that I had a feeling something was going to happen—what, I didn't know. The unusual part of this is that I was typically the last one out of my bunk in the morning.

We left for practice and spent most of the day sharpening our tank skills. We used most of our ammunition doing this. At our base we were told to refuel the tanks and replace the ammunition. Besides all the guns on the tank, there were hand grenades and boxes of bullets for the machine guns tucked around the turret. Under the steel floor was a compartment containing more ammunition. Inside the turret, I found a smoke round stowed incorrectly, and when I went to put it in the right place, I noticed that part of it was loose. (A smoke round contains phosphorus and is

After the explosions stopped, Ernie's tank was towed to a rice field, where it was left until the fire burned out.

designed to create a smoke screen when it explodes.) I wasn't concerned at the time because we had been taught the round was "bore safe," meaning it was safe until it was shot out of a gun.

I attempted to re-stow the smoke round, but when I slid it into the compartment, it exploded in my hands. This explosion set off other ammunition in the tank. Somehow, I got out of the tank through the co-driver's hatch. I yelled, "Clear the tank park!" and passed out. When I awoke, someone told me not to sit up because they were dragging me under a barbed wire fence. I was put into an ambulance and taken to a field dressing station where I was given a strong drug. Then I was taken to a field hospital, where they cut away the burned clothing that remained on me after the explosion. Soon I was in an operating room. What the doctors did, I don't know, but they were surprised that I hadn't been blinded or killed by the explosion. After I healed, I had a low tolerance for heat, and loud noises bothered me. I took medicine for my nerves for a while. Other than that, I was very lucky—or maybe I'm like a cat with nine lives!

Some time after the operation, I was visited by several high-ranking officers, who asked me what had happened. I learned that while I was being taken to the hospital, some of the fellows thought the explosions in the tank had stopped, and they began to get into the tank. But the explosions and fires started again. A sergeant grabbed a man in the turret by his tunic and threw him to the ground. He saved the man's life

On their way home. At the end of the war, Ernie Romans (right) and a friend ride a troop train from Vancouver to Montreal.

and got an MID (Mentioned in Dispatch). The tank was towed to a rice field, and the fire burned itself out.

While I was in the hospital, John returned from his R and R and visited me. He was very upset that I had burned his tank, but we remained friends until I was discharged from the army in October 1954.

One last thing: When you're far from home, you don't expect to see people you know. When I was a kid, my nickname was "Sonny." One day when I was about seven, I was throwing rocks and badly cut a boy's head. Years later, as I was leaving Korea to go home, I was standing near the camp gate and a group of replacements came marching by. All of a sudden, I heard someone calling, "Hey! Sonny!" I looked up. No one in Korea knew that was my nickname as a kid. One of our replacements was the boy I'd hit with the rock!

What refreshment would you offer the president of the United States if he visited your outpost? Charles Davis and his fellow soldiers offered a cold drink from their ingenious cooler.

A Unique Cooling System

CHARLES DAVIS

I was stationed in Korea after the war was over with A Company, First Battalion, Twenty-first Infantry Regiment, Twenty-fourth Infantry Division, and often I would fill in for soldiers who were away on R and R at an outpost called OP Martini. It was north of the Imjin River on the demilitarized zone (DMZ). My job was to sit in a tower on top of a mountain and look through an artillery scope. I was to spot the Chinese soldiers on the other side of the DMZ and report as to whether they were armed or unarmed, what they were doing—that sort of thing.

There were two soldiers on duty at each tower: one man on the ground and the other man in the tower. If the war had erupted again, we would have been the first to die, because we were sitting in full view on top of a mountain.

The tower and our living quarters were very cold because the temperatures could plunge to twenty or thirty degrees below zero. Sometimes it was so cold that the diesel

Charlie Davis spent many hours in this rickety wooden tower at the end of the war, watching over the DMZ.

fuel in the lines for the heaters froze during the night. And imagine going to the screened-in, unheated outhouse. It was best to wait until a couple of other men went before you and got the frost off the seat.

The Chinese were about six hundred yards to the north of the tower, so it was difficult to see if they were carrying weapons. But they were digging tunnels into the mountains. We could see the piles of dirt getting larger and larger.

We were rationed two cans of beer per day while we were at the DMZ. We drank it warm when the weather was warm, cold when the temperatures dropped. Soldiers have a knack for making life a little easier under harsh conditions, and some creative men came up with a system to cool drinks.

At OP Cherry Herring, there was an underground spring, and its water was pretty cold. One of the men had someone in the motor pool at company head-quarters cut a fifty-five-gallon drum so that it had a false bottom. The drum was placed under a piece of metal that directed the cold water into the drum. The drum was buried so that it looked as though it was just an inch or so under the ground, but really it was nearly two feet under.

Cans of beer were placed in the bottom of the drum, and then the false bottom was placed on top of the beer. Then soda—actually, some of the first canned Coca-Cola—was placed on top of that. It looked like there was only soda being cooled in the drum.

When President Dwight D. Eisenhower visited the outpost in 1955, he com-mented on the ingenuity of the cooling system. One of the men then asked, "Would you like a can of soda, sir?"

Little did the president know what was under the soda. Or did he?

The bartering of goods and services often helped both the Allied forces and the people living in the war-torn countryside. Les Funk recalls how the navy kept its vessels shipshape.

The Fruits of Labor

LES FUNK

I was assigned to the USS *Stoddard DD566* for three years beginning at the end of the Korean War. The *Stoddard*, known to the crew as "the Steamin' Demon," was a Fletcher-class destroyer. Its primary combat duties were offshore bombardment with five-inch guns and antisubmarine warfare with torpedoes, depth charges, and hedgehogs. It also provided antiaircraft defense with three-inch guns.

While I was assigned to the *Stoddard*, our homeport was San Diego, California. We were rotated to the Western Pacific Seventh Fleet for a tour of duty that would last five to seven months. The operations with the Seventh Fleet took us across the Pacific to Australia, then north to the Sea of Japan, and on to patrol duty in the China Sea and South China Sea.

Sometimes, after being on patrol in the Formosa Straits (now called the Taiwan Straits), we would steam into and anchor in Hong Kong Harbor. What a busy place

Les Funk emerges from a hatch.

Hong Kong was—with boats, junks, and ships of all sizes, and flags from all around the world flying from their masts.

Because combat ships have to be ready to move quickly into action, the *Stoddard* was rarely tied up to a pier. Instead, we anchored in the harbor so we could weigh anchor to answer a call of duty.

On several visits to Hong Kong, a woman known as "Mary Soo" and her crew of women came out to the *Stoddard* to clean and paint the sides of the ship. Her crew of workers varied in number, but usually there were three or four small boats known as "bum boats" with as many as four women in each. The women scrubbed the ship first, removing old, chipped paint and rust. Remember, the salt and motion of the rough seas do damage to ships, especially when they've been at sea for months.

After the cleaning, the women painted the ship with red lead and a primer. Then they applied new haze-gray paint that made the ship look new again. The women's efforts saved the ship's deck force endless hours of work.

The *Stoddard* wasn't the only ship Mary Soo's crew cleaned and repainted. Other captains in the Seventh Fleet hired the crew to renew hundreds of ships. But Mary Soo's employees weren't paid cash for their work. They were paid in navy food.

Mary Soo arrived with two crews, the painters and the food collectors. The second crew was allowed to board the ship and was escorted to the mess deck, the dining area of the destroyer. After each sailor finished his meal, the women scraped the

A crew of women in their crowded bum boat scrape and repaint a huge ship.

leftovers into individual containers that they had made and brought aboard. Some of the sailors took extra large helpings or went for seconds so there would be plenty of leftovers for Mary Soo's crew. Ordinarily, the leftover food would have been thrown overboard into the sea.

The containers were made of five-gallon rectangular cans with the tops cut off. The cans were called "gunboats" and originally came with vegetables in them. Wire handles made of clothes hangers were attached to the cans. When the women finished cleaning off the trays, and sometimes adding leftovers from the galley, the second crew carried the cans back to their boats and headed to shore. There, they repacked the food and sold it. Everyone benefited from this arrangement: the ships were kept in good repair, and Mary Soo's crews earned food for their families when it was scarce.

Destroyers were the smallest combatant ships of the fleet, with a full battle crew of 325 men. Imagine the leftovers available when Mary Soo's crew repainted a larger cruiser or battleship that held more than 1000 men! After all these years, I still wonder what became of Mary Soo and her painting crews.

Many years ago, a World War I veteran told me, "Son, a veteran's work is never done." He didn't explain just what he meant. Over the years, I have come to realize that the continuing work is remembering and honoring the sacrifices of brave men and women in the past as well as those who currently preserve and protect our freedoms.

After nearly two years in Korea, Lee Philmon returned home to find a little girl who was afraid of him. Who knew that bottles of Coca-Cola would end up satisfying them both?

Welcome Home?

LEE B. PHILMON

My daughter Karen was only six weeks old when I left for the Korean War. When I arrived home twenty-three months later, my wife hurried to the bedroom where Karen was fast asleep. She began to awaken her, although I objected because it was two o'clock in the morning.

As Karen awoke, her mom said, "Daddy's home!" The little girl looked up at me, then looked at a large photograph of me on a nearby table. She started to cry real hard. Her mother tried to tell her that I was Daddy, but to no avail. Karen just cried and tried to hide under her covers. When I moved away, she stopped crying.

I understood—somewhat. Karen had been told repeatedly that the man in the photograph was her father. So who was this stranger who came so near? But understanding did not ease the ache. I wanted to hold and comfort her. No one got a lot of sleep the rest of that night.

For the next two days, Karen reacted the same way whenever I came near her. She cried and hid behind her mother or her grandparents, who were visiting. My wife kept telling her that I was her father, but Karen shook her head and said no. On the third morning, as I walked into the kitchen to join the family at breakfast, Karen cried once again, and my wife began to scold her. "Don't do that," I said, and I picked Karen up, turned, went straight to the car, and put her inside. She moved away from me, crying her heart out. As I drove away, I could see the rest of the family standing on the back porch, watching.

I drove out into the country and stopped at a small store. My daughter was still looking at me and crying. I wasn't sure what to do next. Finally, I got out of the car,

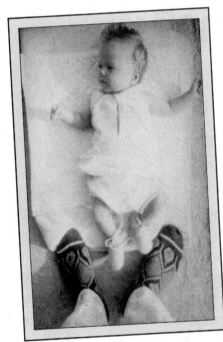

Karen Philmon, six weeks old in 1951. (Daddy's wearing some interesting socks!)

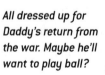

All dressed up for Daddy's return from the war. Maybe he'll want to play ball?

110

went inside the store, and bought two bottles of Coke. I offered one bottle to Karen. She took it and backed away, looking hard at me. I went back inside the store and explained the situation to the clerk, who was looking very concerned. While we were chatting, it suddenly got quiet. "She's quit crying," said the clerk. I raced out the door and hurried to the car.

I could see Karen in the car, in the same place she'd been earlier, only now she was looking intently down the neck of the Coke bottle. She heard my footsteps, raised her head, and looked at me with her beautiful blue eyes.

Lee Philmon

"It's dirty, Daddy!" she said.

Those were the sweetest words I had ever heard.

I smiled at her and said, "Here, take mine." Karen smiled at me as we made the swap, and I went back inside the store. I told the clerk all was well, paid for the two drinks, and went back to the car. As I sat down, Karen scooted over next to me and said, "I like Coke, Daddy," and she put her left arm around my neck. I kissed her on the cheek and said, "So I've heard," and we drove home.

Everyone heard us drive up, and they came outside as I took Karen in my arms. As we walked toward them, Karen told her mother, "Daddy got me a Coke." We were a misty-eyed bunch after that. As I ate my breakfast, Karen sat on my knee and talked a mile a minute. From that time on, she was my little girl, and we were never far apart again.

There's more than one kind of survival during and after a war. For Ed Miller and many other veterans of the Korean War, service-time skills helped them begin to build a new life with their families and communities back home.

"I Will Survive"

EDGAR L. MILLER

The word "tour" is a strange one to describe a soldier's term of duty overseas. To a civilian, it sounds as if you are taking a vacation. Even though Korea is known as "the Land of the Morning Calm," I knew that what was ahead for me was not going to be a peaceful and relaxing journey, no matter what time of day it was.

I was from a small coal-mining community—Logan, West Virginia—and when I received my "greetings" from Uncle Sam, I was still just a kid. Married for only a few months, I left my wife and did what I had to do—I joined the U.S. Army. After basic training in Kentucky, I was sent overseas to Korea. The war was almost over, but it was still my duty to follow the orders as they were issued.

Leaving the United States was by no means a pleasant experience. My final U.S. destination was to be Fort Lewis, in Washington. I was snowbound in Minnesota, but

Home away from home. Edgar Miller decorated his bunk with pictures of his wife, some mosquito netting, a bottle of after-shave, and a radio.

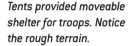

Tents provided moveable shelter for troops. Notice the rough terrain.

the weather finally cleared enough and I was able to reach the fort. I wouldn't be on American soil again for many months.

I was "beached" at Inchon, on the western side of Korea, on the Yellow Sea. From the beach, I made it to a train that traveled north, and when it stopped, I was near the 38th parallel. Imagine: I was thousands of miles away from home, but still on the same latitude as West Virginia.

I was with the Fourteenth Combat Engineers, Company A, I Corps, Eighth Army. My MOS (military occupational specialty) was in supply. The military has to maintain a very large inventory of ammunition, spare parts, replacements, and other supplies, like clothing. Keeping the military's supply system operating smoothly is an important job. There was a lot of paperwork to be done. I received, stored, recorded, and issued supplies.

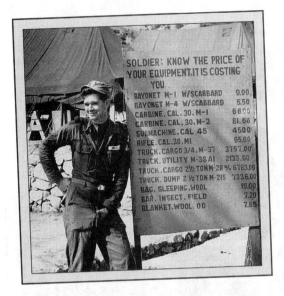

Edgar Miller stands beside a sign that reminds the soldiers that the government can't provide an endless supply of... supplies. At such prices, the soldiers had to be responsible.

When I arrived in Korea, I was not the supply sergeant, the person who issues the authorized supplies, but it didn't take long for me to get a promotion into that position— sergeant first class. I even had a typewriter then. I did what I had to do to keep supplies coming. Sometimes I traded items with our allies. This bartering kept supplies available to our troops.

When you're thousands of miles away from home and at war, the days seem to be never-ending and blend one into the next. My main source of entertainment was a short-wave radio that I bought from a soldier who was going back to the States. I was able to listen to the Voice of America, a government radio service that still broadcasts in fifty-three languages to people around the world. I was also able to receive a radio station in San Francisco. Even though it wasn't my hometown, it was America, and the station brought "home" to me as I listened. When my time in Korea was over and I could return home, I sold the radio to another GI.

Photographs and letters from my wife were precious communications. I pinned the photos of my wife on the wall near my bunk. After the war, I settled into civilian life. I bought and ran a successful business until my retirement. I was also the mayor of the town we live in. My experiences working in supply for the U.S. Army enabled me to manage both a business and a small town.

Even though I still don't like to talk about my time in Korea, I have to admit it is a part of me. I met people from different countries and from all walks of life. We were all strangers bound together by the war. I learned what the word "survive" means, and to this day, I catch myself saying, "I will survive."

Donald Chase (center)

Unwanted Memories

DONALD A. CHASE

Often when I sit alone, and twilight fills the sky,
I find myself recalling scenes from other years gone by.
Memories of Korea still clutter up my head,
Those dreary days and hellish nights, and my friends, long dead.

The many hills we fought through, which never seemed to end,
And all the while the fear inside, of death around the bend.
The clashes with the enemy, who sometimes fled away,
But, for every hill we won, someone had to pay.

Maybe one was lucky, when a bullet found an arm;
For a little while, at least, you were safe from harm.
My mind recalls the icy weather, when diseases took their toll,
When frozen feet were common, from winter's numbing cold.

115

The trench line with its bunkers and grimy faces there
Where if you were observant, you saw the burnt-out stare.
The pathway from the trenches that led to no-man's land,
A torn and barren piece of ground, destroyed by human hand.

Always, there were those who fell, never to arise,
And to this day, I still can see the shock in startled eyes.
These vivid pictures locked inside, although they do not show,
Never seem to leave my thoughts, no matter where I go.

A veteran of World War II, Donald Chase re-enlisted in the U.S. Army and served in Korea from early 1951 until October 1953. During that time, he was seriously wounded four times. After each recuperation, he returned to battle. At the end of his service, he was a platoon sergeant in I Company, Fifteenth Infantry Regiment, Third Infantry Division. His wartime souvenirs include the memories captured in his poetry and the bullet that once lodged in his neck, nearly paralyzing him.

Afterword

Korea remains divided today. The Main Line of Resistance, as it was known to the Korean War service members, is now the DMZ, or demilitarized zone. The DMZ is 155 miles long and two and a half miles wide. No military activity can take place in the zone. No military forces can take positions in the DMZ. But they can stand on either side of the zone, watching and waiting. This they have done since the war ended.

As the service members returned home, some a year or more after the war, they were greeted by relieved and happy families but found none of the huge parades and celebrations that had welcomed the veterans of World War II. Over the years, theirs became known as "the Forgotten War." Within their homes and communities, through their written histories and volunteer work with veterans' organizations, they tried to remind the world of the contributions to freedom that they and their fallen comrades had made.

As the fiftieth anniversary of the beginning of the war approached in 2000, more attention was paid to their accomplishments. Construction began on the Korean War Veterans National Museum and Library in Tuscola, Illinois. The veterans' constant pressure upon agencies to help them locate some of the thousands of those listed as missing-in-action has had increasing success, too.

Over the years, the U.S. Army has had access to sites to locate some of the unaccounted-for American war dead and repatriate them. Recovery missions have brought home service members located in South Korea. In 1996, the United States negotiated with the Democratic People's Republic of Korea to allow the U.S. Army Central Identification Laboratory in Hawaii (CILHI) to visit battlefields in North Korea to collect the remains of U.S. service members. Since then, search-and-recovery teams have battled bad weather and rugged terrain in remote sites to recover remains and transport them to the CILHI at Hickam Air Force Base in Hawaii for identification. Dental records and DNA samples from the soldiers' families help the teams identify as many of the men as possible. After positive identification, the remains of service members are returned to their families for burial with full military honors. Many, like the Krepps family (see pages 82–86), still wait in the hope that their loved one will be found and returned to them.

The United States is committed to "leaving no one behind." However, it is not always possible to bring everyone home. Many of the UN troops from around the world are buried far from home in cemeteries in Korea and Hawaii.

Since the war, South Korea has experienced brighter times with greater economic strength and the world's recognition—for instance, during the 1988 Olympics, which were held in Seoul. Veterans who return find rebuilt, flourishing cities and villages where once there were ruins.

Meanwhile, North Koreans, led since 1994 by Kim Jong Il (son of Kim Il Sung), have suffered from famine and a poor economy. Tentative cross-border exchanges have meant happiness for some Korean families reunited after fifty years, but the constant threat of renewed nuclear-arms production in North Korea makes the unification of North and South Korea a distant, if not impossible, dream. By early 2003, Korea was in the daily news again as the North Korean government ignored the

United Nations and began to reactivate its nuclear facilities. "It breaks my heart to see all of this tension in Korea again," said one Korean War veteran.

Permanent peace in "the Land of the Morning Calm" remains a goal. "The Forgotten War" signs and bumper stickers are being replaced by those reading "I Remember Korea." Participants in the Korean War, through their recorded memories, share with us the history and the humanity of one time in the world's story. They help us realize that, truly, "Freedom is not free."

Time Line

June 25, 1950

North Korean soldiers cross the 38th parallel and invade South Korea.

June 28, 1950

Seoul, the capital of South Korea, is captured by North Korean forces.

July 1, 1950

The first U.S. ground-combat troops arrive in Korea.

July 5, 1950

The Battle of Osan, first U.S. ground action of the war.

August 4–September 16, 1950

North Korean forces are stopped when the United States and South Korean forces set up a defensive perimeter around the port city of Pusan, South Korea.

September 15–16, 1950

American forces land at Inchon, South Korea.

September 15–30, 1950

United Nations troops break out of Pusan Perimeter and recapture Seoul.

November 25, 1950

The Chinese army enters North Korea, and UN forces are pushed back from the Yalu River.

November 27–December 9, 1950

The Battle of the Chosin Reservoir takes place, and UN forces are surrounded.

December 24, 1950

UN forces are evacuated from the North Korean city of Hungnam.

January–April 1951

Chinese forces push the UN troops back across the 38th parallel. Seoul is recaptured by the Chinese.

February 13–15, 1951

The Battle of Chipyong-ni occurs, the first mass assault by the Chinese Communist Forces (CCF).

February 16, 1951–July 27, 1953

The Siege of Wonsan, the longest siege of a port in U.S. Navy history, lasts 861 days.

April 11, 1951

General Douglas MacArthur is relieved of his duties as UN Commander by President Harry S. Truman. Lieutenant General Matthew B. Ridgway is appointed the new commander.

April 22–29, 1951

The First Spring Offensive is fought—the largest single battle of the Korean War.

April 24–26, 1951

During the Battle of Kap'yong, UN troops successfully defend a four-mile-wide valley and repel the Chinese forces advancing toward Seoul.

May 1951

UN forces again recapture Seoul.

May 30, 1951

The Battle of Chail-Li.

July 10, 1951

Peace talks between North Korea and UN forces begin.

August 18–September 5, 1951

The Battle of Bloody Ridge is fought.

September 13–October 15, 1951

The Battle of Heartbreak Ridge.

November 27, 1951

The two sides agree on the 38th parallel as the line of demarcation; fighting slows down but does not end.

July 17–August 4, 1952

The Battle for Old Baldy.

August 12–16, 1952

The Battle of Bunker Hill.

October 26–28, 1952

The Battle of the Hook occurs.

November 29, 1952

President Dwight D. Eisenhower flies secretly to South Korea.

April 16–July 10, 1953

The Battle of Pork Chop Hill.

April 20–May 3, 1953

"Operation Little Switch" is carried out. By agreement, Chinese and Korean prisoners are sent back to North Korea, and South Korean and UN prisoners are sent south. The exchange is made at Panmunjom.

July 24–26, 1953

The last U.S. ground combat takes place.

July 27, 1953

Representatives of the United Nations and North Korea sign an armistice at Panmunjom. The war ends, but a permanent peace treaty is never signed.

August 5, 1953

"Operation Big Switch" begins. Over the following six weeks, almost twelve thousand prisoners are returned by the Communists. The UN forces return more than seventy-five thousand prisoners to the Communists.

July 27, 1995

The Korean War Veterans Memorial is dedicated in Washington, D.C., by President William J. Clinton. Other Korean War memorials have been built all over the world.

October 17, 1998

President Clinton signs Public Law 105–261. Section 1067 declares that the "Korean Conflict" will henceforth be called "The Korean War."

2000–2003

Ceremonies marking the 50th anniversary of the Korean War are held around the world. Among those honored are the men and women who returned from the war, and those service members and civilians who lost their lives.

Countries that participated in or contributed noncombatant services to the Korean War:

UN Forces:
Australia, Belgium, Canada, Colombia, Denmark, Ethiopia, France, Greece, India, Italy, Luxembourg, the Netherlands, New Zealand, Norway, the Philippines, South Korea, Sweden, Thailand, Turkey, the Union of South Africa, the United Kingdom, the United States.

China and North Korea

These nearly life-sized figures at the Korean War Veterans Memorial in Washington, D.C., seem to move silently across the shrubs and granite "water." The Lincoln Memorial rises behind them.

In another view of the Memorial, the soldiers are mirrored in the commemorative wall that rises beside them.

Glossary

active duty—performing the services assigned or demanded for full pay.

artillery—troops trained to use and service large mounted weapons.

battalion—a military unit, usually consisting of a headquarters company and four infantry companies or a headquarters battery and four artillery batteries.

bazooka—a portable weapon consisting of a long metal tube for firing small armor-piercing, explosive rockets at short range.

bivouac—a temporary encampment made by soldiers in the field.

boot camp—a training camp for those who have joined the armed forces (so called because the recruits wear boots, not shoes).

Bronze Star—a U.S. Army decoration awarded for heroism or achievement in ground combat.

C rations—cold food, usually in cans (now called MREs–Meals Ready to Eat).

cannoneer—a gunner or artilleryman firing cannons.

CIA—Central Intelligence Agency, the agency that coordinates U.S. federal intelligence activities.

CILHI—the U.S. Army Central Identification Laboratory Hawaii. It is made up of about 250 military and civilian personnel under the command of a U.S. Army colonel, but it employs military personnel from all branches of the armed services. They recover and identify the remains of service members from World War II, the Korean War, the Vietnam War, and other conflicts.

commission—an official document issued by a government giving an individual the rank of a commissioned officer in the armed forces.

company—part of a regiment or battalion.

decommissioned—no longer authorized to perform certain duties.

depth charges—a quantity of explosives designed to explode under water after being dropped or catapulted from a ship's deck; used against submarines.

division—an administrative unit that directs troops, is self-sufficient, and is equipped for long periods of combat.

DMZ—(demilitarized zone) a region, determined by diplomatic agreements, where no military forces or buildings can be placed. In the case of Korea, the DMZ is located at the North Korean–South Korean border.

fatigue cap—cap that is part of the fatigues, or clothing designated or permitted for military work or field duty.

field kitchen—a portable kitchen set up where troops are camped.

flak jacket—a thick nylon vest worn by ground troops. Weighing about eight pounds, it protects the back, chest, and middle abdomen from shell and hand grenade fragments and low-velocity missiles.

flame thrower—a weapon that projects ignited fuel in a steady stream.

GI Bill—legislation whereby, after World War II, veterans were given government assistance in order to study at college or university.

GI—an enlisted man in, or veteran of, any of the U.S. armed forces. Originally the abbreviation for "galvanized iron," an army clerk's term for items such as trash cans; later said to be the abbreviation for "general issue" or "government issue."

guerrilla—member of a movement made up of small bands fighting to undermine the enemy.

headquarters—the military offices from which official orders are issued.

hedgehog—an explosive device propelled underwater to its target; its shape looks like a hedgehog, hence its nickname.

honey bucket—container for human waste.

houseboy—usually orphaned Korean boys; they performed tasks for the soldiers—made beds, cleaned boots, washed clothes—and were clothed, fed, and paid by the soldiers.

infantry—the branch of an army made up of units trained to fight on foot.

intelligence—the work of gathering secret information about an enemy, or the office that does such work.

junk—a Chinese flat-bottomed ship.

KIA—killed in action.

martial law—temporary rule by military authorities imposed upon the civilian population, usually in a time of war.

MASH—Mobile Army Surgical Hospital—a movable hospital set up in tents.

med evac—medical evacuees; the wounded removed from the field.

MLR—Main Line of Resistance; today called demilitarized zone (DMZ).

no man's land—the field of battle between two opposing armies.

Nuremberg Trials—After World War II, charges were brought against twenty-two Nazi leaders. The International Military Tribunal tried them in Nuremberg, Germany, between November 20, 1945, and September 30, 1946.

parallel—an imaginary line running parallel to the equator that represents a degree of latitude.

Pentagon—a five-sided (pentagon-shaped) building in Arlington, Virginia, where the U.S. Department of Defense is housed.

pilot house—an enclosed area on the deck of a ship; the ship is controlled by crew in the pilot house.

platoon—a subdivision of a military company divided into squads or sections.

POW—prisoner of war.

provisional—temporary.

Purple Heart—the U.S. armed forces' medal of the Order of the Purple Heart, awarded to service members wounded in action; features the profile of George Washington on a purple-and-gold background.

R and R—rest and recreation; some leisure time away from the battlefield; often spent in Japan during the Korean War.

reconnaissance—a survey of an area performed to learn about its terrain or the possible placement of military forces.

regiment—a military unit of ground troops consisting of at least two battalions .

repatriate—to return to the country of one's birth or citizenship.

reserve—a trained fighting force kept inactive until needed.

Semper Fidelis—Latin for "Always Faithful"—the motto of the U.S. Marine Corps.

separation—discharge from military service.

Silver Star—a U.S. military decoration awarded for gallantry in action.

spinal—a spinal anesthetic.

squadron—a basic military unit consisting of two or more groups of aircraft, divisions of a fleet, or troops.

tinsel—metal foil dropped to interfere with antiaircraft weapons.

troops—uniformed military personnel.

unit—a group that is part of a larger group; a particular group of soldiers.

WIA—wounded in action.

Further Reading

Chorlian, Meg, ed. *The Korean War 1950–1953* (Peterborough, New Hampshire: Cobblestone Publishing Company, 1999).

Giesler, Patricia. *Valour Remembered: Canadians in Korea* (Ottawa, Ontario: Veterans Affairs Canada, 1990).

Hastings, Max. *The Korean War* (New York: Simon & Schuster, 1987).

Highsmith, Carol M., and Ted Landphair. *Forgotten No More: The Korean War Veterans Memorial Story* (Washington, D.C.: Chelsea Publishing, Inc., 1995).

McCune, George M. *Korea Today* (Cambridge, Massachusetts: Harvard University Press, 1950).

McGowen, Tom. *The Korean War* (New York: Franklin Watts, 1992).

A Pocket Guide to Korea (Washington, D.C.: U.S. Government Printing Office, 1950).

Web Sites of Interest

www.koreanchildren.org—The Korean War Children's Memorial, in Bellingham, Washington

www.koreanwar.org—Korean War Project

www.kvacanada.com—The Korea Veterans Association of Canada Inc.

www.kwva.org—Korean War Veterans Association

http://Korea50.army.mil—Official public access web site for the United States of America's commemoration of the Korean War.

www.womensmemorial.org—Women in Military Service for America Memorial

www.theforgottenvictory.org—Korean War Veterans National Museum and Library

Index